ON STAGE WITH SMILIN' BILL AND KING

*The more I read it, the more I love this book.
It's a winner.*

Editor Peggie Painter

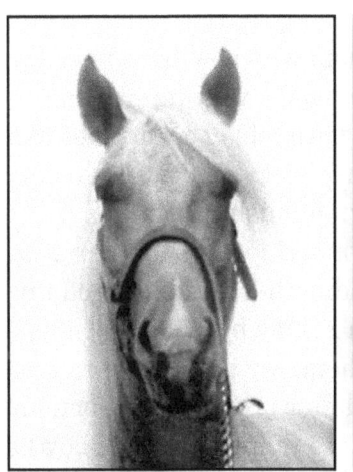
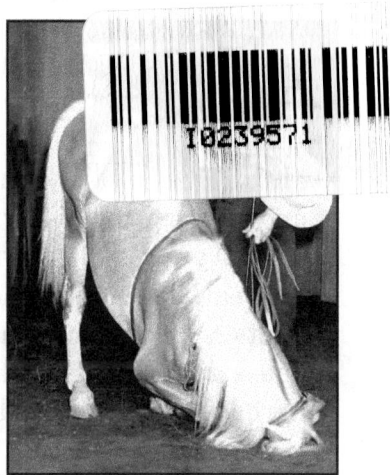

King says, "I'm listening" and "I'm praying."

King Greets the Audience with a Kiss

*A successful book is not made of what is in it,
but what is left out of it.*

Mark Twain

TRIBUTE
BILL CUMMINS — PROUD TO KNOW HIM

Bill Cummins is my cousin who now lives near Daytona Beach, Florida. He lived a very interesting and sometimes sad life, with lots of good times. After retiring, he began writing books on life and history and even started his own publishing company.

Bill grew up dirt poor and lost his mother at a very early age. My grandmother, Mildred, and my aunts helped them each Friday by cleaning their house and cooking for them. My grandmother was his dad's sister. Bill had four brothers, if I remember right. They scratched out a living with each boy having to pull his own weight.

Bill had a Wild West show for years, or at least until he could go to college and earn a degree in engineering. I could go on about him for hours, but it would take weeks to tell all about him. I am very proud to call him my family. His wife, Ann—she is a sweetheart, and I am happy they found each other.

I remember "King" when he was performing with Bill. He lived to a very old age for a horse. My hat is off to cousin Bill Cummins, and I recommend all of his books. They tell the genuine truth.

Jeffery Roberts, Texas, September 18, 2010

KING
and the
COWBOY

The Saga of "Smilin' Bill" and his Wonder Horse "King"

~ A TRUE STORY ~

WILLIAM A. CUMMINS

CAI Publishing
Port Orange
Florida
"Home of Celebrity Authors"

KING and the COWBOY
The Saga of "Smilin' Bill" and his
Wonder Horse "King" — A True Story

© 2011 by William A. Cummins

ISBN-13: 978-0-9787766-8-8
ISBN Print Edition: 0-9787766-8-2
ISBN PDF eBook Edition: 0-9787766-9-0

Published by CAI Publishing
807 Black Duck Drive, Suite A
Port Orange, FL 32127-4726, USA
Website: http://www.caipublishing.net
Email: info@caipublishing.net
Office: 386.383.5198

All rights reserved. No part of this book may be reproduced or transmitted in any form or by any means, electronic or mechanical, including photo-copying, recording or by any information storage and retrieval system without written permission from the author, except for the inclusion of brief quotations in a review.

Cover Photo: "Smilin' Bill" and his Wonder Horse "King" performing in the majestic Schines Holland Theatre in Bellefontaine, Ohio, prior to their opening act onstage that evening, which headlined the first Western show ever to emanate from Logan County as the *Diamond J Ranch Round-Up*.

Printed in the United States of America Library of Congress Control Number: 2011905601

Copyediting by Peggie Painter/M.Ed.
Interior artwork by Ann Cummins
Design and layout by Martha Nichols/aMuse Productions®
Cover design by John Morris-Reihl/Art and Technology

THE HORSE

THE HORSE...a living, breathing animal, soft of eye, curious of ear, skin twitching to dislodge a fly!
                                               Author Unknown

The 2010 motion picture *Secretariat* begins like this:

More than three thousand years ago a man named Job complained to God about all his troubles and the Bible tells us God answered, saying

> *Do you give the horse his strength or clothe his neck with a flowing mane? Do you make him leap like a locust, striking terror with his proud snorting? He paws fiercely, rejoicing in his strength, and charges into the fray. He laughs at fear, afraid of nothing; he does not shy away from the sword. The quiver rattles against his side, along with the flashing spear and lance. In frenzied excitement he eats up the ground; he cannot stand still when the trumpet sounds.*
>
>   *Job 39:19-34 NIV*

SECRETARIAT developed from a foal into one of the greatest race horses of all time. KING developed from a foal to a proud, majestic stage horse. **Destiny!**

DEDICATION

> *This book is a tribute to the unselfish talents of my friends Montana Frank and California Joe and their ability to teach others the secrets of show business.*

The cowboy and his faithful steed are etched into the minds of countless millions of people around the globe. Working together they symbolize the spirit of independence and freedom unequaled in the human experience.

This book is a testimony to this bonding of horse and rider. May it never die away or be forgotten in the hearts of people who love and cherish freedom. But freedom comes with a price, which led me to this dedication.

Let me begin by dedicating this book to the men, women, and children who long ago left their homes and fought against nature and human odds to conquer the Old West. They faced hardship and death to seek freedom and independence.

Next, this book is dedicated to our veterans and soldiers who are our first line of defense. They are the dauntless men and women who still cherish the Old West traditions of honesty and hard work. They stand ready to defend our freedom wherever they are needed.

Finally, this book is dedicated to each and every man, woman, boy, and girl who has ever gazed in awe upon this magnificent animal...perhaps one of God's greatest gifts to mankind!

EPIGRAPH

*Horses — if God made anything
more beautiful, He kept it for Himself.*
                          Author Unknown

KING and the COWBOY is not a book about how to make your horse a "beast of burden." Instead, it will provide a blueprint for fundamentally changing your beliefs about man's best friend.

Here are some things you will learn:

- How a horse can touch and enrich your life
- Why trainers must learn "Horse Sense"
- The secrets of a simple lesson in trust
- Why real cowboys do not pull leather
- Three rules for training a horse to perform successfully on stage
- How to make quick and correct decisions every time you work with your horse
- How to memorize and write Western songs
- The secret of the four-hour workday
- Two things you must do instinctively if your horse rears over backwards
- Why trick roping needs hands-on training
- And much, much more…

ACKNOWLEDGMENTS

Inspiration

I am especially grateful that God fulfills the dreams of all who dare to dream big dreams. Time alone will reveal the truth of what God is doing through us and for us as we pursue our dreams.

Vision

Gene Autry was the single vision set forth by all the movie cowboy heroes during my youth. He wrote the "Cowboy Code," which reinforced my moral conduct and ethical beliefs. This was especially valuable to me since I did not attend church until after age 21.

Trust

My parents, Robert and Ruth Cummins, started me on a steady course through life. They taught me to trust and believe "Right will always win out." Lew Jenkins moved me from tenderfoot cowboy to expert when he trusted me to run his riding ranch.

Support

Most importantly, I express gratitude to my wife, Ann, for her boundless patience, faith, assistance, and encouragement during the researching and writing of this book. My special appreciation also goes to Peggie Painter for her careful editing, helpful commentary, and seamless phrasing offered during the completion of the book.

PRELUDE

King was a beautiful golden palomino stallion. He and I headlined as "Smilin' Bill" and his "Wonder Horse "King." Looking back, I realize just how special our coming together was for both of us.

As a teenager with a big dream, I was given the job of training King for the stage. Lew Jenkins, his owner, offered me the job as his Diamond J Ranch manager when I was 15 years old.

It was a full time job during the summer months at a riding stable located in a famous resort in Ohio. If you truly love and understand horses, you will feel my youthful excitement when given this opportunity.

In order to explain how I developed training techniques and produced an incredible stage routine with King, I must begin with the simple boyhood dream of becoming a cowboy movie star.

Also shared is how this boy became a man through the many personal trials and setbacks that occurred before his horse training skills were perfected. With a lot of hard work, King became one of the finest stage horses ever seen. He was King the Wonder Horse.

> *My horse-training techniques were developed*
> *by learning to think like a horse.*
> *They worked for me*
> *and they will work for you!*

DISCLAIMER

This book is based upon the author's experiences and relationship with King the Wonder Horse. It is sold with the understanding that the publisher and the author are *not* attempting to redefine the true art of horsemanship.

If legal or other expert assistance is desired, you are invited to pursue your interests in other venues. Resources by other competent horsemen should be sought by anyone interested in more information. It is not the purpose of this book to reprint information otherwise available.

Horse training is not a skill to be taken lightly and requires serious handling to be successful and safe. Books, therefore, are not a substitute for the personal guidance of an experienced horseman.

Every effort has been made to make this book as accurate as possible. However, there may be both typographical and content mistakes. Therefore, the text should be used only as a general guide and not as the ultimate source of information.

The purpose of this book is to educate, entertain, and inspire. The authors and CAI Publishing shall have neither liability nor responsibility to any person or entity with respect to any loss or damage caused or alleged to be caused directly or indirectly by the information in this book.

If you do not wish to be bound by the above, you may return this book to the publisher for a full refund.

TABLE OF CONTENTS

Introduction and Overview xiii
CHAPTER 1—Onstage with Bill and King.... 1
CHAPTER 2—Everything Is First a Dream... 17
CHAPTER 3—A Shredder Ate My Fingers ... 25
CHAPTER 4—No Trigger Finger —
　　　　　　　No Service.................. 31
CHAPTER 5—Death Knocked at Fifteen 35
CHAPTER 6—The Singing Cowboy 41
CHAPTER 7—Running the Ranch 47
CHAPTER 8—I Was Boss, but He Was King.. 53
CHAPTER 9—California Joe, King, and Me .. 57
CHAPTER 10—A Spinning Rope
　　　　　　　　Seems to Float 63
CHAPTER 11—Diamond J Ranch Road Show. 73
CHAPTER 12—Ditch the Psychiatrist Couch . 81
CHAPTER 13—Cowboys Do Not Pull Leather. 85
CHAPTER 14—300 Miles on Horseback...... 91
CHAPTER 15—Just Call It Horse Sense 101

CHAPTER 16—A Simple Lesson in Trust 107

CHAPTER 17—Think Like a Horse 113

CHAPTER 18—Breaking Up Is Hard to Do ... 121

CHAPTER 19—The Last Goodbye 125

CHAPTER 20—Without Heroes 129

AFTERWORD—Gene Autry Was My Hero 137

APPENDIX A. Gene Autry's Cowboy Code..... 138

APPENDIX B. King's Breastcollar
Preserved................... 139

APPENDIX C. I'm Gonna Ride that
Trail to Heaven 140

APPENDIX D. Why Do Cowboys Wear
High Heels?................ 141

APPENDIX E. An Old Cowboy's Tombstone ... 142

APPENDIX F. Resources................... 143

APPENDIX G. Other Books by Author........ 144

Quick Order Form......................... 145

INTRODUCTION AND OVERVIEW

The article below was published in the April 1985 edition of *Inside Malcolm Pirnie*. Bill was regional manager of the Columbus, Ohio, office of Malcolm Pirnie, an environmental engineering consulting firm situated in White Plains, New York.

THE SAGA OF "SMILIN' BILL" AND HIS WONDER HORSE "KING"

Bill Cummins picked himself up by the bootstraps, literally and figuratively.

Although well spoken and self assured, Bill still maintains a country boy approach as a seven-year member of Malcolm Pirnie's management team.

No wonder! This Columbus engineer, a licensed professional engineer in six states and a student of Ohio State University's Graduate School for Sanitary Engineering, was born and raised on a

William A. (Bill) Cummins Corporate Photo 1985

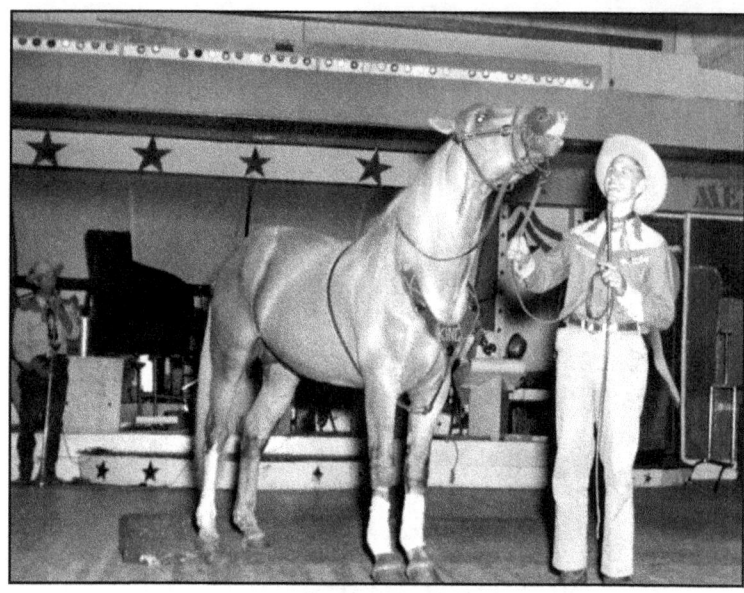

farm in Ohio. He cooked meals on a wood stove for his widowed father and four brothers, while aspiring to be a country-and-Western singer and radio star!

Bill acquired his first pony when he was six years old, his first guitar when he was ten. His hero was Gene Autry!

In his sixteenth year, Bill's music repertoire included over 300 songs, many of which he was the composer and lyricist. He had his own Saturday morning radio show, and stardom was on the horizon!

By his late teens, Bill was adept at breaking and training Western horses and trick roping. He trained a Palomino Stallion to do stage tricks, formed a country and Western band and headlined shows across the state of Ohio. "Smilin' Bill and his Wonder Horse King" were on their way!

During this adventuresome time, Bill traveled 300 miles on horseback, from his hometown in Ohio to Chicago, Illinois, sleeping under the stars for eight days and enjoying the life of a cowboy alone with his horse.

In time, Bill gave up "show biz," took a full-time job with an engineering firm and married. His entertaining talents were shelved, save for his own amusement.

Bill and Phyllis Cummins settled down to a quiet family life, raised three children, Kathryn, Alanna and Alan and remained active in church activities while Bill continued his engineering studies for eight years.

Thirty years after Bill retired his guitar and boots, his hidden talents were unearthed by Sid Zeid and Mike Macy of the Columbus office.

In 1981, when the Columbus office hosted a Christmas party for twenty prestigious guests, Bill was called upon to perform rope tricks! Completely surprised by the request and out of practice for many years, Bill was further amazed to find he had not lost his touch. His routine was as smooth and professional as it was decades ago! Bill ended his performance by roping and tying up the Service Director of the City of Columbus, Bob Parkinson.

The following year, Bill's talents were again enlisted and, guitar in hand, he sang the familiar country and Western tunes of so many years ago!

Bill's ambition and persistence resulted in his ultimate success—as a performer and an engineer. The Engineering Manager in Malcolm Pirnie's Columbus Office has been invited by the Governing Board of the Ohio Section of the American Water Works Association to perform at President Dick Miller's reception in Washington, D.C., this spring.

As Bill Cummins says, he is living proof of the old saying, "You can take the boy out of the country, but you can't take the country out of the boy!"

Chapter One

ONSTAGE WITH BILL AND KING

SMILIN' BILL AND HIS WONDER HORSE KING

I was 15 years old when I first met this gangly two-year-old palomino colt named King. During the next three years, I matured into a young entertainer

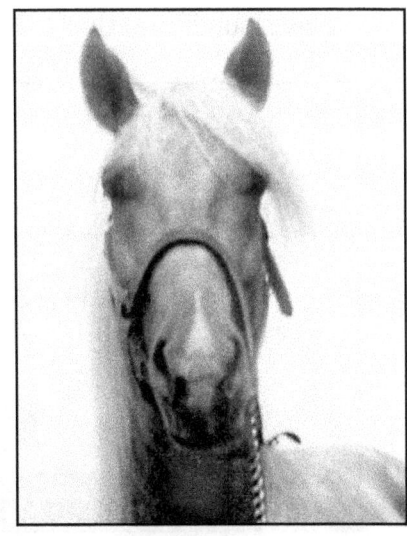

Smilin' Bill and his Wonder Horse King

known as Smilin' Bill. The colt became a beautiful golden stallion known as King the Wonder Horse.

During those three years we forged a lifelong bond as I taught him how to become a star. When we took the stage, all eyes were upon him. My mission was to make King appear larger than life on stage with an effortless professional routine that would amaze and entertain the audience.

"Smilin' Bill" and his Wonder Horse "King" was the banner headline of our Western road show. We developed the acts and organized the show during the late 1940s. The show originated from a bustling resort known as the Sandy Beach Amusement Park located in Russells Point, Ohio.

The Sandy Beach Amusement Park was located along the southern shoreline of Indian Lake. Before closing in 1975, it was celebrated across the nation for more than 50 years as "Midwest's Million Dollar Playground" and the "Atlantic City of the Midwest."

Sandy Beach Roller Coaster and Ferris Wheel

Our stage show rehearsed and later performed at the famous Old Vienna Gardens night club. The club was located in the midst of the Sandy Beach Amusement Park amid many dance pavilions and ballrooms filled nightly with patrons.

When our show appeared at the Old Vienna Gardens, King and I entered through the club's front door, not through the club's stage door. The crowd would be sitting with drinks in hand at small tables around three sides of the large stage. We were required to pass directly through the club patrons, so close they could reach out and touch us from their seats.

When appearing at the majestic Schines Holland Movie Theatre in Bellefontaine, Ohio, we entered through a narrow winding stairway behind the stage. King was a large horse and had to twist and squeeze his body around the tight turns as he followed behind me. I often worried about him, but he trusted me to keep him safe and unharmed.

Looking back, I was lucky to get top billing for the show as Smilin' Bill. I was only a young starry-eyed kid with big dreams. King was a beautiful palomino stallion who looked a lot like Trigger, the famous Hollywood horse ridden by Roy Rogers.

Before each show I carefully bathed King with Prell shampoo to make him smell fresh and clean. I braided his long white mane and white tail to make them wavy and brushed him from head to tail to make his golden coat glisten under the stage lights.

With those preparations accomplished, we were ready to travel to the show. Upon arrival, I backed

Unloading King for the Show

King from the trailer and signaled him to go to the bathroom. The audience really did not want to see a "King" size accident on stage.

It was show time, and we both were anxious to move onstage. King's rubber horseshoes muffled the sounds as we moved toward the entrance. I patted his neck and whispered, "King, you look great." We both felt the tension increasing. I could see his skin ripple slightly as his ears flipped back and forth.

He was unsaddled and fitted only with a stylish red bridle with reins attached to a large silver bit in his mouth. Buckled around his neck was a wide, red leather breastcollar. I could see his name "KING" in the middle of his chest and the initial "K" made of small silver conchos on each side of his neck.

King's name and initial(s) were highlighted by large silver conchos. The red leather color brought out the gold in King's coat and the conchos sparkled in the stage spotlight. The breastcollar was secured with a short leather strap passing between his front legs and attached to a narrow red leather surcingle fastened around his girth.

I was dressed in an appropriate Western outfit with polished brown high-heeled boots, a white hat, and I carried a short leather riding crop in my hand. When the stage was set, I jumped onto King's back and gave the thumbs up signal that said, "We're ready."

Standing on stage dressed in Western attire was the Master of Ceremonies, Lew Jenkins. He had rolled out a large padded canvass mat to protect King's body from the hard wooden floor during the show. Lew placed my lariat behind the mat, strolled to the microphone on stage right, and signaled the band to start the theme song.

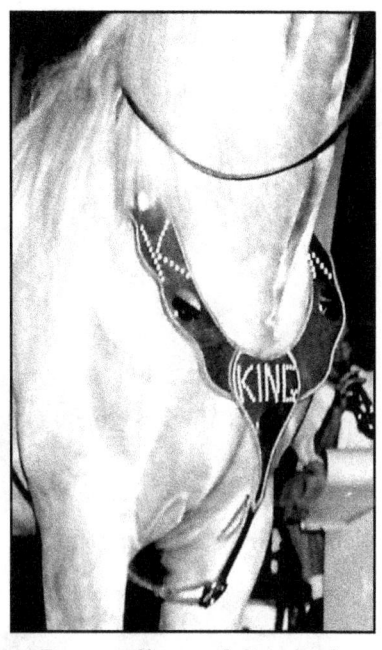

Breastcollar and Surcingle

"California, Here I Come" blasted loudly across the showroom from the live band behind the stage. Waiting through several bars of music, Lew began his introduction.

"Now ladies and gentlemen for your pleasure... and entertainment...please give a warm welcome to our stars...who will delight and amaze you. It thrills me to present to you...Smilin' Bill and his Wonder Horse King!"

The band played louder as we quickly made our way toward the stage during the applause. Sitting

Parade Stretch — Training Photo

Kneeling Pose — Training Photo

astride King, I guided him to center stage.

I turned him stage left into a Parade Stretch before turning him toward the crowd into the bright lights. I could feel King's excitement as his soft skin rippled again and his ears shot forward.

He stood quietly as I dismounted on his left side. I smiled and with my riding crop touched King's left front leg. At my touch, he knelt by bending his left leg to the mat. I removed my hat and bowed my head, which elicited even more applause.

As I replaced my hat, King stood erect and our eyes met briefly. He was ready for the show.

Lew began the show with, "King, the audience gave you and Smilin' Bill a very nice reception. Why don't you throw them a kiss in return?" I could feel King's left eye watching me for a cue. He wasn't nervous as long as I was in his line of sight.

Standing near his head at eye level, I tilted my head up and lifted my riding crop vertically in my left hand while holding his left rein in my right hand. All eyes were on King as he lifted his head up and curled his upper lip showing his teeth in what looked like a kiss and a smile.

We needed to break the ice quickly and connect with the audience.

A Kiss and a Smile at the Old Vienna Gardens

If the audience response was too slow, I'd cue him to do it again. When they showed their approval, the rest of the show could proceed.

Lew picked up the pace, "King, do you like the crowd today?"

Without moving, I signaled King to nod his head up and down in a big "Yes" motion two times.

Lew smiled and continued with, "That's great, King. They tell me you are very smart; is that true?"

King again nodded his head "Yes."

"Okay, do you mind answering some questions for this audience?"

I patted King's neck, and at the same time, lifted my forefinger toward his shoulder. He shook his head almost like a shiver as he said, "No," much to Lew's surprise.

"I'm sorry, King, don't you feel well?"

King again shook his head "No."

When the crowd laughed loudly, I knew we had a good audience that would enjoy the rest of the show.

"Are you having problems with your girlfriend?"

King nodded his head, "Yes."

"Do you want to talk about it?" asked Lew.

"No," said King.

The head of a horse looks naturally sad and this gesture looked sincere to the crowd. A slight murmur came from the ladies in the crowd as King's ears shot forward.

Sensing sadness from the crowd, Lew asked, "Is she a pretty filly?"

King twice nodded, "Yes."

"Did she run off with another handsome horse?"

King again nodded, "Yes."

Lew then dropped his voice to a low whisper and said, "Do you want to go beat him up?"

King waited a couple of seconds as if thinking it over. Then slowly shook his head, "No."

"Well then, did something change your mind?"

King nodded, "Yes."

"Was it another pretty filly?"

King nodded his head "Yes" several times.

Lew said, "Now that's what we humans would call horse sense."

The crowd applauded and cheered.

"King, I've also heard you know how to count."

Seeing my left foot move forward, King lifted his left front foot a couple of times in a pawing motion while nodding, "Yes." I shifted my foot back, he stopped.

Lew continued, "Then tell the crowd how old you are."

I cued King to count five times with his left leg, and the crowd approved the act with their applause.

"King, do you know how old I am?" asked Lew.

"Yes," he nodded.

"Do you think you can count that high?"

King nodded "Yes," so Lew continued, "Do you think we have time to do it right now?"

King twice shook his head, "No," and the crowd roared.

"That's enough, King," said Lew. "Now let's turn to your math skills. How much is...two plus five?"

King responded with seven leg counts.

"That's right! Can you also subtract four from 13?"

King nodded "Yes" and pawed the stage nine times.

"King, have you also learned how to divide?"

When King nodded, "Yes," Lew said, "Then divide four into 20 for us."

This time I cued King to overcount to nine instead of five. The crowd moaned at King's error, and Lew looked shocked.

"King, I asked you to divide four into 20. Do you want to answer the question again?"

King nodded, "Yes," and this time he correctly counted to five.

When he stopped the crowd applauded approval.

"Well, King, the only thing left is multiplication. Can you do that, too?"

King twice nodded, "Yes," and began to paw.

Continuing, Lew said, "It looks like you can't wait for this question. How much is...three times four?"

Pausing, as if thinking about it, King then counted to 12. I removed my hat, and the crowd applauded loudly.

"Well done, King. Now let's change the pace and show these nice folks how you walk on your knees. I know it isn't easy, so take only a few steps."

I turned King in front of me until he faced stage left. Then I leaned over touching the leather crop to both of King's front ankles.

After he gently dropped to his front knees, I led King forward across the stage mat. He took five short steps with his hind quarters high in the air. The crowd loved it and showered him with applause.

King stayed on his knees as Lew said, "King will now do a Camel Stretch while Smilin' Bill stands high in the air on his hind quarters."

I touched King's chin with the crop, and he stretched his chin as far forward as he could on the floor. Walking behind him, I jumped onto his hind quarters. Then I stood erect about 11 feet in the air. When I removed my hat, the applause began again.

As I dismounted from King during the applause,

Camel Stretch on Stage at the Holland Theatre

I heard Lew explain, "Bill and King always have a Prayer Time during each show. They consider it one of the most important parts of the show."

During these tricks King had held his position on his knees. I walked quickly to his left shoulder and picked up the reins. When King felt the gentle tug of the reins, his head moved back between his front knees until his face was flat on the mat in a praying position.

I removed my hat and bowed my head as the crowd applauded one of my favorite stage moments. I could tell King's knees were beginning to hurt from the stress of performing three tricks in succession.

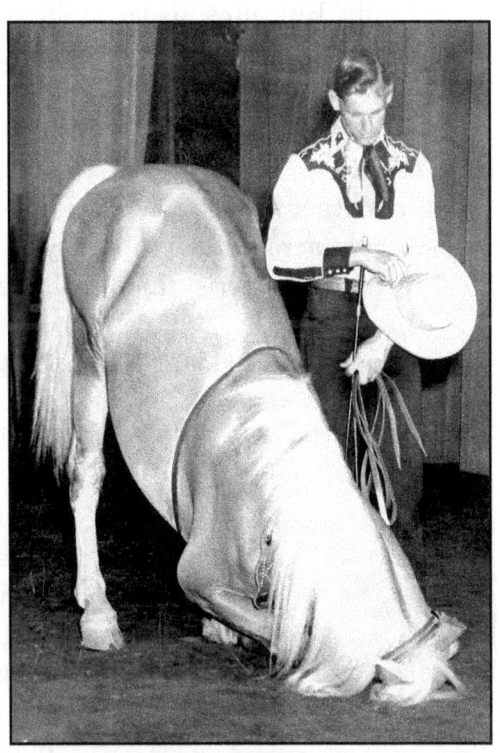

Prayer Time with King and Bill

Before proceeding, I stroked King's shoulder to let him know everything was going well. His ears flipped back and forth to say he understood.

I touched his side with my crop and he gently dropped his hind quarters onto his left side and slowly lowered his head onto the floor mat.

Lew said, "King is tired. We'll let him rest while Smilin' Bill spins his lariat for you."

I picked up my 50-foot spinning rope from the floor behind the mat. Holding the coil of rope in my left hand, I shook out a small loop with my right hand.

With a flip of my wrist, I spun the loop from left to right across the front of my body a few times, by reversing my wrist. Lew explained this was called a Butterfly Loop.

Stopping suddenly, I flipped the long coil of rope in my left hand out across stage left. King lay quietly on the floor watching me as I opened a large loop with my right hand.

Spinning 50-Foot Rope While Standing on King

He didn't flinch as I stepped on top of his right front shoulder with my left boot. Stepping forward I placed my right boot gently onto his rib cage.

My high heeled cowboy boots were painful to King's skin and muscles, so I quickly twirled the rope into a loop around my body. Then I pushed it larger and larger until all 50 feet of rope was circling in a large loop around King and me.

When I slowed the spinning rope, King knew it was time to get up. I dropped the spinning rope to the stage floor and stepped off of King's side.

As the applause began, King lifted his head from the mat and drew his front legs under him. Picking up his reins quickly, I stopped him while he was in a sitting position facing the spotlights.

I removed my hat to more applause. Watching me intently, King moved immediately as I touched his hip with my crop and said, "Get up, King."

King drew his powerful hind legs under him to stand up. In one quick motion, I swung my right

King Sitting Up — Training Photo

leg over his back and rode him to a standing position. It was quite dramatic, and it happened so quickly that the audience would gasp loudly in admiration. I stayed on top of King for the rest of the show.

Lew regained the full attention of the audience by saying, "King will now perform a Cake Walk for you by switching his front feet as he lifts them high in the air and kicks them forward."

Cake Walk — Training Photo

I placed my right boot near his front shoulder and gently tugged the right rein along his neck to start the first strut. We moved from side to side for about five steps and stopped. I patted him along the neck as they applauded. King and I enjoyed the applause, the stage, and the spotlights, but we knew we were approaching the end of the show.

Lew said, "A cowboy's life is lonely and hard. At day's end, both the horse and rider are very tired." I moved forward on King's back while loosening the reins and touching his left shoulder with the crop.

As his head dropped near the floor, I removed my hat, leaned forward with my head down, and with my legs I nudged King's hind legs forward until they were near his front legs.

We stood motionless for about 15 seconds as Lew

The End of the Trail — Training Photo

explained, "This is a famous pose called The End of the Trail. It is a favorite of many Western artists."

"However," he said forcefully, "the most famous image of a cowboy is when a horse triumphantly lifts his rider high in the air while standing on his hind legs. Bill and King will salute you now as the show ends."

Squeezing my legs against King's sides, I pulled back on the reins and said, "Up, King." This cued King to move forward and back up at the same time.

Salute — Training Photo

He reacted by lifting his front legs and body high in the air in a beautiful gesture. I held King in this erect pose for a few seconds before letting him drop again to the stage.

Lew ended the show, "Thank you for being a wonderful audience." I touched King on the left shoulder with my riding crop. He curtsied as I removed my hat one last time while applause thundered throughout the audience.

"California, Here I Come" blasted again

Curtsy Pose — Training Photo

from the band as we headed offstage through the crowd. I could feel King's excitement under me.

King knew he had performed well. I was proud of him too and often wondered what tall tales he would tell the stable mares. Wouldn't you like to be a fly on the wall and listen?

I toured with King for three years and really enjoyed that part of my life. I will forever treasure all those memories. My passion for horses has never faded, especially for "King the Wonder Horse."

Bill and King — Pals Forever

Chapter Two

EVERYTHING IS FIRST A DREAM

Everything is a dream until you make it real.
William A. Cummins

My world was filled with horses from my very first memory. Why not? I was born when farming was still done with horses. I can remember when our first tractor showed up a few years later.

The country roads were covered with gravel or dirt. Our farm had no electricity, running water, or plumbing, and wood was our only fuel for cooking and heating. You can see a similar lifestyle in many Amish farm communities today.

I was the middle child of five boys. We all arrived during the first seven years of the great worldwide depression. I am eternally grateful that abortion had not been legalized when we were born, although Dad and Mom would never have considered it.

We were all born at home, just like 95 percent of the community. Doctor V. F. Barrett from Lakeview, Ohio, took care of birthing most of the kids in our area. Cash was scarce back then. So scarce I was told that Dad gave chickens and eggs to Doc Barrett for delivering each of us.

When we were very young, we helped gather eggs from the hen house. Later, we carried small buckets of water to the farm animals. Each year as we grew older and stronger, more chores were added. There was, however, plenty of time for daydreaming and playing together between our morning and evening chores.

Watching Dad work with his team of horses and seeing his fondness for them instilled in me the same love and respect he demonstrated. He loved to work with them and was proud of how well they worked together. I watched those 1,500-pound draft horses obey Dad's voice commands without hesitation.

Attached to their bridles were two long leather lines Dad held in his hands. His voice commands were *giddy up, gee, haw, whoa, steady, move over,* and *back up*. He patted them on the neck to show his approval.

It wasn't long before I was petting and leading them in the barnyard. I played around and under them without fear. They seemed to enjoy the games and Dad made sure they never stepped on me.

I learned their tickle spot was in the flank area near their hind legs. A rippling of their skin and a stomp of their legs soon taught me that if you want horses to get irritated, just touch them on the flank.

Dad believed if you take good care of your horses, they will take good care of you. Even as a young lad, I realized there was a very special bond between humans and horses. I believe now that the horse is God's most outstanding gift to mankind.

Dad thought bicycles were unsafe on the farm. He believed riding them on the dirt paths and gravel roads was too dangerous, so he decided to get us boys a pony instead. Nothing could have pleased us more.

Soon a medium-sized pony showed up and we immediately named him Brownie. What a thrill for us. It didn't take us long to learn how to feed, water, brush, put on his bridle, and ride.

Since Brownie never had a saddle, learning how to fall off our bareback pony was one of the most valuable lessons we learned. Brownie, unlike a bicycle, would come to a stop if he thought we were falling off.

Bill Singing to Brownie, his First Pony

As we grew taller, it became time to transition from a pony to a horse. That is also about the time I began admiring the taller horses the cowboys rode in the movies. But let me explain how it happened because the fun is in the details.

Dad rented our farm from a couple of business men in the nearby county seat. One of the owners brought a tall horse named Major to stay on the farm for his twin boys to ride when they visited.

After riding Major, it didn't take long for me to decide I preferred the taller horse to the pony. After all, the movie cowboys rode tall horses.

A couple of years later, Dad traded Brownie for a taller horse and a saddle. She was a glassy-eyed Welsh mare named Dolly. Her coat was mostly white with splashes of light red over her body.

My job with Brownie and now with Dolly was rounding up the cows twice a day for milking. Both animals were gentle with us boys as we rough-housed daily around the farm.

Bill and Bob astride Dolly

One of Dad's farming rules was, "Everything has to pay for its keep by producing something of value." He applied the rule to our ponies and to our pets.

I was five when a little terrier dog wandered into our yard. Dad agreed to let him stay only after he proved he would eagerly catch rats around the barn. That little dog became our first pet. We named him Popeye because of the black circle around one eye.

Dolly was no exception to the "earn your keep" rule. She was mated with a palomino stallion and a few months later produced a beautiful filly. I was 12 years old at the time, and she was the first colt I cared for and trained by myself.

I named her Speedy, and we became best friends. As a young nursing colt, Speedy stayed with Dolly in one of the stalls in the barn. After feeding Dolly one morning, I turned to leave. Like a child wanting to play, Speedy reached out and grabbed the left cheek of my small rear end with her teeth.

It didn't hurt much at first, but when I tried to turn around and escape her grasp, the pain shot all the way up to my head. I knew her jaws would close before opening again, so I painfully pulled my tender butt cheek from between her clenched teeth.

When I heard her teeth snap shut, I turned around to scold her. Then I saw her playful eyes begging me to nip at her. She thought it was a game colts played with their friends.

Dolly was watching cautiously as she munched on her grain. As the awful pain in my butt slowly subsided, I patted Speedy to let her know I wasn't mad at her. But thereafter, I always watched my behind when she was near.

Speedy had a light golden coat and a small white diamond on her forehead. Although smaller than Dolly, she was formed so well that as a two year old, she won first prize in the conformation category at the big Logan County Fair.

I was very proud of her and the way she acted during the contest. She strutted proudly with head and tail high as I led her past the judges during the show. I think we were both show-offs that day.

On Saturday nights during the summer months our family would drive into town to watch the free cowboy movie. The local creamery produced them free in order to draw a crowd. Dad gave each of us a dime to buy ice cream.

The movies were shown outside on the side of a white building. When I saw one of the horses in the movie answer questions by shaking its head, I got excited and began to wonder if Speedy could learn to do something similar.

Dad would never teach his farm horses to do stunts, so I had to figure out how to teach Speedy by myself. I asked everyone I knew, "How do you teach a horse to do tricks?" No one I knew could tell me.

One day I was eating an apple as I played with Speedy. She watched me and started hunting for the apple in my hand. While teasing her with the apple core, I moved it up to the side of my face.

When she reached up and nuzzled my cheek, I released it to her lips, and she munched it gleefully. After repeating it a few times she began nudging at my cheek on her own and begging for apple bites.

Every time I raised my hand and said, "Kiss" she would reach up and nudge my cheek. Soon she began doing it on command. WOW! I did it! I taught Speedy to kiss me on the cheek.

This little trick worked so well that I wanted to try another, but had no clue about what to do. One day I met a neighbor who had trained his horse to answer questions by nodding his head up and down for

"Yes" and shaking it sideways for "No," as well as to count by pawing with his left front leg.

What a thrill it was when he showed me how to teach Speedy. It wasn't long before we were both showing off to everyone who would watch.

At this point, you can see where my dreams were heading. But there were some serious setbacks I had to overcome along the way. Setbacks we will cover in the next two chapters.

*You can lead a horse to water,
but you can't make him drink.
You can lead a boy to class,
but you can't make him think.
To make the horse drink,
lead him into the stream.
To make a boy think,
lead him into the dream."*

—Anonymous

Chapter Three

A SHREDDER ATE MY FINGERS

Let's start by taking a look at my first grade picture at Washington Township School in Lewistown, Ohio. Our teacher, Mrs. Truax, in back row center, taught 44 beginners, but only 23 graduated 12 years later.

Washington Elementary School. Young Bill Cummins is fifth from the right in the first row.

All went well until I reached the fourth grade. The only picture I have with the thumb and index finger on my right hand is shown in the photograph taken by my fourth grade teacher, Jewell Fullerton.

Pictures were rare during the Great Depression and Miss Fullerton photographed every student who passed through her fourth grade class. Following her death, a big stash of her pictures was discovered and returned to her students as keepsakes.

You must admit I was a handsome young lad all dressed up in hand-me-down clothes from two older brothers. I even wore a belt and suspenders. Take a good look at the picture because a few months later, I severely injured my right hand in a farm accident.

Bill before Right Hand Injury

The accident happened in the fall season of my ninth year as I tried to help the family gather in the shocked bundles of corn from the fields. It was an accident that altered my life.

The shocked bundles of corn were hauled to the barnyard by wagon and hand fed into a mechanical monster called a corn shredder. The big machine was driven by a belt connected to a monstrous farm tractor parked a few yards away.

Chapter 3 A Shredder Ate My Fingers

It was a full-time job to align the thick wide belt from the tractor to the corn shredding machine and keep it running. Starting and stopping the shredder was not easy and everyone tried to keep down time to a minimum.

The Corn Shredder Was a Big Noisy Monster

The corn shredder ripped the ears of corn from their stocks and removed the husks by pushing them through serrated steel rollers. The stocks, leaves, and husks were shredded into fodder and blown into the haymow of our barn. The fodder became feed and bedding for our livestock during the winter months.

The shucked ears of corn exited from the side of the machine and dropped through a chute onto a short mechanical conveyor which moved them up into the wagon and dropped them into a pile.

My job was to stay in the corn wagon and shovel the ears of corn to the back while Dad fed the stalks of corn into the shredding machine from the field wagon. Occasionally an ear of corn got stuck coming out of the husking rollers onto the conveyer.

When it first happened, I yelled for my cousin who was helping us that day. I watched him unplug the ears a couple of times. Then I decided to climb down from the wagon and do it myself. Twice I was successful, but the third time was tragic. It happened

Shredder with Shredded Stalks on the Ground

in a flash as the husking rollers grabbed my glove.

Before I could snatch my hand back, the rollers pulled my small hand into the rollers and mangled the ends of my thumb, forefinger, and middle finger. The tangled glove, mixed with skin and flesh, hung down from my right hand like twisted spaghetti.

When I saw the blood, I became frightened and started running toward the house. As I ran, I had to lift up my hand to keep the dangling skin and flesh from dragging on the ground.

While running to the house, I remember feeling disappointed in myself for not staying in the wagon as Dad had instructed. However, I was just a nine-year-old kid trying to help Dad with the farm work.

Mom saw my hand when I ran into the kitchen. She immediately lifted the bloody mess and plopped it into a wash basin of clean water she had prepared for the dinner meal.

She ran as fast as she could to the barn to fetch Dad who was unaware of the accident. I stared at the awful looking mess of flesh in the wash basin as the water quickly turned red.

While Dad shut the shredding equipment down, Mom wrapped my hand and arm in a clean netted window curtain from her linen drawer.

Chapter 3 A Shredder Ate My Fingers

Dad asked my cousin to drive us to the doctor's office, which was about 15 miles away. As he drove his new Ford sedan, I kept saying, "Drive faster! Drive faster!" We sped like crazy over those narrow hilly roads towards the doctor's office. I was scared and getting more and more anxious with every mile.

Dad held my arm as we walked quickly into the office and operating room of Doctor Charles Barrett (Dr. V. F. Barrett's son). I climbed onto the operating table and lay down on my back. I watched the nurse carefully unwind the curtain from around my arm.

When the mangled fingers appeared, she gently lifted my hand and placed it onto a white linen cloth covering a small surgical tray that was attached to the side of the operating table.

While I lay there staring at my hand, the lights went out as my thoughts slowly melted from reality into the peace of darkness.

When I awoke, it was dark outside. The surgery was over, and my hand was neatly bandaged with white gauze and saturated with a strange smelling ointment. After seven decades, I can still remember the smell of that ointment and feel the mangled twisted flesh of that hand.

The healing of my partially amputated index and middle fingers went fairly well. However, my thumb was amputated at the first knuckle and the skin had been removed by the machine rollers. The remaining flesh turned black and had no sign of life in it.

Young Doc Barrett feared that I might lose my thumb. His hope was to generate new life back into the blackened flesh. He decided to use a new medical procedure involving ultraviolet light radiation.

Twice a week I visited his office where my hand was unbandaged and treated for 15 minutes with the ultraviolet light. Then my hand was bathed again in that strange smelling ointment and rebandaged.

Thank God the ultraviolet radiation worked. The flesh slowly turned pink and skin began to grow. My dad said young Doctor Barrett was very proud of his work. I am very thankful that he saved my thumb.

Chapter Four

NO TRIGGER FINGER — NO DUTY

As a child, I did not realize how much my partial thumb would mean to me later in life. Now it seems like a miracle. Without the aid of a stub thumb, my dreams of becoming a singing cowboy entertainer would have vanished.

I do not even want to think about what my life would have been like without the thumb on my right hand. Without it, I could not play the guitar, spin rope, write, dress, or perform the myriad of other activities I learned to do very well.

Before the accident, each of us had to milk two cows by hand twice a day as part of our daily chores. While my hand was healing, I kept hoping Dad would say, "Bill, you don't need to milk the cows anymore."

My hopes were dashed, however. Dad assigned me to my regular farm chores as soon as I was able to squeeze my hand tightly. He gave in just a little bit, because he let me milk the cows with large teats. My four brothers were kind and never complained.

Looking back, the exercise of milking by hand every day was the best thing he could have done for me. This therapy worked the same as squeezing a rubber ball and gave me strength in my right hand.

Thanks to Dad's wisdom and work ethic, I didn't lose the use of my right hand. Even now, I only notice the missing fingertips and end of thumb when I try to button a shirt or pick up small pins or coins. I quickly shift the task to my left hand.

Although the accident happened when I was only nine years old, it did affect my adult life. Ten years later the horrific Korean War began in 1950. I tried to enlist but I was rejected from duty because of the missing trigger finger and thumb on my right hand.

I often wonder what direction my life would have taken if I had served. It certainly would have altered my life. Personal stories of the Korean War are best described by Veterans in Volume One of my award-winning book, The Forgotten.

Dick, my oldest brother, was married with a family when the war began and was not called into service. He died in 2006 following a long struggle with lung disease in DeGraff, Ohio, where he lived with his wife, Colleen (Morris) Cummins.

Jack, my older brother, served aboard a Navy destroyer off the Korean peninsula. He switched to the Air Force and retired in good health after 20 years of service. Twice married and divorced, Jack lived in Yuma, Arizona, where he died in 2009.

Brother Vern enlisted in the Army and served in Japan during the war. He retired at the end of his enlistment, married Carol (Gardner), and raised a family in Kenton, Ohio, where he died in 2008 after a severe stroke.

My youngest brother, Bob, enlisted in the Air Force. He was stationed at a radar installation in Alaska during the war. Bob retired at the end of his enlistment, married Judy (Tait), and raised a family. He lives on a small farm in Enfield, North Carolina.

Dick (left), Vern, Bob, Bill, and Jack

These photographs of my brothers and me were taken shortly after the Korean War began. I am dressed in cowboy garb; Jack is in his Navy Whites, while Dick, Vern, and Bob are dressed in farm attire.

We worked hard and played hard but never got into any trouble while growing up. We worked seven days a week on the farm. Since our parents did not attend church or join any social organizations, we had only the friends found at school.

At age 18, I was headlining on stage as a cowboy singer and entertainer. Then at age 20, I invited God into my life. Shortly thereafter, I married a beautiful lady, Phyllis (Holycross), and started a family.

I joined my wife's church, and our great pastor, Richard Baker, led me into an active ministry as a teacher, church leader, and lay speaker within the United Methodist Church.

During those years, while working full time, I studied engineering courses from the International Correspondence School and attended courses at the Kenton High School, and Ohio Northern University. Later, I studied graduate engineering courses at Ohio State University.

At 29, I registered as a professional engineer and later moved to Columbus, Ohio to begin a career as a consulting environmental engineer, a career that lasted nearly 50 years.

After retiring, I began to write and established CAI Publishing to provide celebrity authors with salient professional services. A list of my books and a quick order form are noted in the appendices.

Chapter Five

DEATH KNOCKED AT FIFTEEN

Tragedy is no respecter of time, person, or place and my family was unprepared for what happened next. Following the hand injury, my life moved along rather smoothly until I was 15 years old. We lived on rented farms and had moved to nearby DeGraff, Ohio as World War II was ending.

Robert E. Cummins; Ruth R. Cummins
Dad — Retired Farmer; Mom — Graduation

Dad was in his late sixties when this picture was taken. Mom's picture was taken at her High School graduation in 1926 at Lewistown, Ohio. Her maiden name was Burden. This is the same 12 grade school I graduated from in 1949.

Washington Township School at Lewistown, Ohio

My parents grew up in the Northwest part of Ohio and were married in 1928. They rented farms in several places around Indian Lake while raising a family during the great depression. Their big dream was to have their own farm someday.

Dad was 45 and Mom reached 40 before they had saved enough money to make a down payment on a farm. They chose a beautiful homestead located near Lewistown, Ohio. In the 1800's, a wealthy family had built a historic two story brick home on the property.

The house had been built on a hill overlooking a river on the east and a huge barn and outbuildings

Chapter 5 Death Knocked at Fifteen

New home on the hill; Main entrance (right)

on the west. We moved to our new home the first day of January 1947, and I settled into a new school routine with new neighbors and plenty of chores.

I do not remember Mom complaining about being sick until Dad rushed her to the hospital. We went to bed on January 19th thinking Mom would be home the next day. On the 20th, our relatives awakened us five boys to tell us our mother had died during the night.

I buried my face in my pillow crying, "No! No! No!" It felt like my world had ended. In a very real sense that was true. All I remember is shock, anger, unbelief, and sadness. I felt life would never again be safe, secure, or innocent. Sometimes, life can deal you a knockout blow.

Mom's funeral was only a blur, with relatives and friends trying to console Dad and all of us. Dick had just turned 19, Jack was 16, I was 15, Vern 13, and Bob was 11. Dad was wise to keep us together, but some immediate challenges followed. I had no idea what was in store for me.

Since I had never shown any serious interest in farming, Dad appointed me the chief cook and bottle washer for the Cummins' clan. My new job started immediately. I had to learn how to cook for my Dad and four growing brothers, and I needed to learn in a hurry, before all the donated food was eaten.

This was not going to be easy. Our kitchen had no running water or plumbing. The kitchen stove was a huge iron relic that burned only firewood for heat. That firewood had to be split into small pieces, carried into the kitchen, and shoved into the stove firewell as I cooked. I knew how to chop wood, but cooking was an entirely different matter.

Aunt Mildred, Dad's sister, showed me how to manage the stove and gauge the heat by watching how fast lard melted in our huge cast iron skillet. She taught me how to fry eggs, toast bread with the oven divider, and make Dad's black coffee.

I must have cooked those things for breakfast, dinner, and supper for several weeks because Dad finally said, "Bill, don't you think it's about time you learned how to fry something besides eggs?" I was so busy I never thought about cooking anything else. All of a sudden it hit me, "Wow! Imagine cooking something other than eggs."

Dad asked Aunt Mildred to teach me a few more dishes and before long I was cooking a wide variety of wholesome farm food for the clan. It was so good that our neighbors would ask to stay and eat if they were around at meal time.

Chapter 5 Death Knocked at Fifteen

I guess you never know what you can do until you do it. Before leaving home, I cooked a meal from scratch for over 20 guests on that old wood range.

While attending High School, I cooked only two meals a day, breakfast and supper. Dinner at noon was cooked by my older brothers who had quit school to help with the farming.

All the dirty dishes, pots, and pans from dinner were left for me to clean when I returned home from school. Since there was no hot water in the kitchen, my first task was to start a fire in the wood range and heat the water for clean up.

I learned to sweep the house with a broom, but with school, I had no time for mopping, dusting, or washing all the dirty clothes for six men. Dad again called upon Aunt Mildred for help.

With her help, every Friday became a big treat for us. She would scrub the house, wash the clothes, fix the meals, and bake several delicious pies before returning home. We never forgot about her caring for us that way. It taught us to be grateful, and we loved Aunt Mildred dearly.

It's hard to imagine how much food we consumed every day. I do recall that we butchered two of our own beef cattle and at least four hogs each year. We also ate lots of chicken and wild game like pheasant, rabbit, and squirrel.

If we boys had our way, most of the beef and hogs would have been turned into ground meat. But Dad insisted that we keep some steaks and chops. It may be hard to believe, but bologna from the store was a real treat for us.

With five boys around, Dad decided that to keep us out of the local pool hall, we could have our own pool table. It was a monster table that he found in the community and it took all of us to lift and assemble it in one of the first floor rooms.

This worked out well because we played pool almost every night. In fact, during the next three years we wore out two of the heavy green pool cloths that covered the table.

Dad saved a lot of his money by keeping us home nearly every night. He was a smart man.

Bill's Photograph for High School Graduation

Chapter Six

THE SINGING COWBOY

When I was about ten years old, Dad bought me a second-hand guitar from a local pawn shop. I was very excited and didn't realize how high the strings were above the frets or why that would matter.

    I felt the sharp pains assault my fingertips when I pressed the steel strings down onto the fret board. The pain did not matter, however, because I felt that

Smilin' Bill Cummins, the Young Singing Cowboy

another part of my dream was coming true. I wanted to learn how to play, so I suffered through the pain.

I could not read music and had never picked up a guitar in my life. Luckily, a neighbor, Joe Brubaker, showed me how to strum and play the chords. "Pistol-Packin' Mama" was a popular song at the time, and I decided to learn how to play and sing it. Joe taught the melody to me and showed me the chords as he hummed the music.

Over and over, I would hum and strum the familiar phrase...*dah-dah-dah-dah-daaah-daaah*. Though any experienced musician might laugh, it was tough to do. Again and again, I would strum the chords in their proper order, trying to recreate the melody.

How long did it take me to learn that song? I cannot remember! I believe I have forgotten that detail out of pure embarrassment, but the breakthrough event finally arrived. While practicing at home, I hit upon the melody until I nailed it. I learned how to play and sing "Pistol Packin' Mama."

With that accomplished, I knew I would surely be a singing star in a matter of weeks. That was a huge daydream when my "band" consisted only of Joe and me, and Joe was just learning to play his guitar. My big desire was to sing on The Grand Ole Opry stage and become famous like Gene Autry.

Lacking musical training, I had to memorize my favorite songs by listening to them on the radio. One by one I copied the lyrics and hummed the music. Soon I was writing my own music, and by the age of 17, I had memorized over 300 country/western songs.

Chapter 6 The Singing Cowboy

Nearly all country and western music contains stories related to everyday life. Once memorized, I discovered that I could still sing and play many of the songs decades later. My soul feels refreshed when I remember the past through those songs.

I played the guitar and sang at many events in the local area. I even gathered up the nerve to ask traveling entertainers to let me sing with them on stage whenever they appeared near my home. Since I was basically a shy person, this took all the nerve I could muster.

I won second place in the big Logan County Fair amateur show. At about that same time, I met Cecil Moist who asked if his teenage daughters, Mary and Marsha, could sing along with me.

Bill, with Mary and Marsha Moist and Joe Brubaker

After singing together for a while, Cecil took us for an interview at radio station WPTW in Piqua,

Ohio. In 1948 the program manager, Bill Fox, offered us our own radio show every Saturday morning.

We headlined as "Bill Cummins and the Moist Sisters." I was the Master of Ceremony of the show and had to do all the talking. Those 15 minutes of air time seemed like an eternity. I asked myself, "How should a shy cowboy singer handle this task?"

Showtime: Bill with Marsha and Mary Moist

I decided to copy the relaxing style I admired from a weekly half-hour radio show called "Gene Autry's Melody Ranch." It worked well for our show and our fan mail came from as far away as Canada. We were a radio station hit.

Later on I organized a complete Western band that toured with the Diamond J Ranch Roundup. "The Diamond J Ranch Hands" provided background music for me and for various segments of the show. Although I wrote several songs, they were never recorded and only a few still have written words.

Chapter 6 The Singing Cowboy   45

The Diamond J Ranch Hands: left to right, Norman Williams, Charles Woodell, Lowell Crock, Johnny Green, and Bill Cummins

Bill Backstage at a Rodeo Show

Feed Bucket Philosopher

If you make your horse mind when it is in the barn, it will mind when it is out of the barn.
             Robert E. Cummins (My Dad)

Chapter Seven

RUNNING THE RANCH

When I was 15, something unexpected happened that changed my life. After Mom died in January and I was finishing my sophomore year in high school, Lew Jenkins offered me a job.

He asked me to run his Diamond J Ranch and riding stable located near the famous Sandy Beach Resort in Russells Point. It would only be during the summer break, but what an opportunity!

I was unaware while growing up that Lew had been watching me develop good riding and horse training skills. Though I was still pretty shy at 15, I jumped at the chance to learn more about training horses and riding.

I was both surprised and grateful when Dad allowed me to accept Lew's offer. It meant I would not be home to cook for the Cummins' clan during the summer months. This was a huge imposition on my brothers and Dad, because they had to pitch in and perform my cooking chores during their very busy farming season.

Running the stable was a seven day a week job and kept me hopping from dawn to dusk. There were usually 10 to 15 horses at the ranch. Feeding and caring for horses was not hard for me because I had always done it on our farm.

However, dealing with the inexperienced guest riders was new and challenging. Being alone all day entailed meeting, greeting, teaching, and protecting the riders and horses while overseeing the ranch, stable, and grounds.

Working alone also meant I was responsible for all the cash collected. That was something new for a young kid who had been cash poor most of his life and was now earning $35 a week.

Bill and Friend Wait for Guests to Arrive

We charged each rider $1.50 an hour which was a lot of cash for me to handle. It wasn't unusual to have a cash box full of dollar bills and change by the end of the day.

Each rider had to sign a waiver releasing the stable from any liability due to injury. To further protect the stable as well as each horse and guest, I learned how to take charge of every rider, regardless of their age. After sizing up their skill and attitude level, I was able to match them with a horse they could safely handle.

Occasionally, I mismatched the riders and had to change horses before something ugly happened. On a busy day I had my hands full. I rode along with the riders around a scenic trail behind the stable and barn. My attention was divided as I kept an eye on the riders and still watched for new guests arriving at the front of the stable.

I arrived early each day, usually by 7:00 A.M. I opened the stable and cleaned the stalls before the horses were rounded up from pasture. After feeding the horses, they were brushed, saddled, and halter tied. Their stalls were located along each side of the open driveway through the stable building.

When guests arrived, the horses were bridled and prepared for riding. Matching horse and rider meant dealing with all ages, sizes, and shapes of riders. I taught them to pat the horse's neck and talk calmly to their new friend.

Basic survival techniques were taught to avoid injuries. Leaving nothing to chance, I showed the amateurs how to lead their horse with their right hand and mount from the left side.

Before they mounted, I adjusted the stirrups to match their arm's length and, if necessary, helped them climb aboard. After they mounted, I checked again for proper stirrup length and placed it under the ball of each foot.

I taught them more basics, including how to start with loose reins held in one hand, and say, "Giddy up," along with stern side kicks with their heels to make them go. To stop, they were to pull lightly on the reins and say "Whoa."

They learned to turn the horse by neck reining — that is, pulling the rein against the opposite side of the horse's neck. Finally, I reminded them to kick the horse's sides with their heels to keep them moving while on the trail.

Watching the "Greenhorns" Ride Away

Chapter 7 Running the Ranch

After turning the "greenhorns" loose, I watched closely as they moved out onto the trail. If I noticed any problems, I would mount up and ride along with them until they got the hang of it.

On really busy days, I would spend six to eight hours in the saddle. That left precious little daylight to work on my trick roping skills and King's training for the stage performances he was destined to do. There was little time to rest until the sun was down.

There's nothing so good for the inside of a man as the outside of a horse.

Ronald Reagan

To understand the soul of a horse is the closest human beings can come to knowing perfection.

Author Unknown

Chapter Eight

I WAS BOSS, BUT HE WAS KING

Lew's favorite horse in his stable was a sleek bay mare he named Lady. I'm sure Lew named her Lady because of the fine hair in her mane and tail. It was not because of her lady like temperament. Since she had a quick temper, she needed an experienced rider and was not useful as a rental horse.

Lew and Lady; Bill and Lady

Lady had a soft comfortable stride and was an integral part of the ranch operation. Lew and I depended on her skills and savvy when riding close to others as we chaperoned our riding guests.

At the close of my third summer season at the ranch, she carried me 300 miles on an eight day trip from Ohio to Aurora, Illinois, where I delivered her to her new owner. Lady was a sweetheart to ride.

King, unlike Lady, was a free-wheeling, spirited colt. When I first met King he was too young to ride. Lew had only begun to give him obedience lessons.

It was coincidental that Lew and I used similar methods of horsemanship. However, because of that stroke of luck, I was able to continue expanding King's training without a pause.

This part of my cowboy saga begins with the empowering effect of a young boy's dream. Looking back, I know it was only my unfettered youthful daydreams that brought King and the Diamond J Ranch into my life.

We were both youngsters when we met at the Diamond J Ranch. I saw only a hint of curiosity in King's eyes when I first walked past his stall.

The ranch operation was so new to me that I ignored King when I first arrived at the stables. Looking back, I feel a little guilty for ignoring him. He was seldom ignored, even then, because he was one eye-popping colt.

King was maturing into a tall golden palomino stallion, with a great disposition and an eagerness to learn. He captured my heart the very first moment we began working together and was never ignored by me again.

King was a young three-year-old stallion, and I was a very shy 15-year-old wannabe cowboy. We were a good match for those two reasons alone, but soon we found much more to respect in each other's character.

Lew, King, and Bill Preparing for a Show

King and I had no idea that our first meeting would lead to real friendship and to headlining an amazing first class stage show. It was a show where I was the boss, but he was always King.

Then, one amazing day a traveling troupe of cowboy entertainers arrived. Headlining their show was Montana Frank, California Joe, and Pinto, the Hollywood Trick Horse. That was the day everything changed for us.

The following chapters describe how this troupe impacted everyone at the Diamond J Ranch. Within a short time, the ranch developed into a full blown stage show highlighting unbelievable talent.

King and Lew; King's Private Stall

My dreams came true as King and I matured into professional stage performers that headlined across the Midwest. What a thrill... What a ride... What a story! "Smilin' Bill" and his Wonder Horse "King" were on their way.

Chapter Nine

CALIFORNIA JOE, KING, AND ME

When the student is ready, the teacher will appear.
                              Buddhist Proverb

During my second summer at the Diamond J Ranch, Lew invited a traveling cowboy troupe to stable their stage horse at the ranch while they performed at the Old Vienna Gardens in the resort.

"Montana Frank and California Joe with Pinto, the Hollywood Trick Horse" were featured in their show. Montana Frank had mastered the Australian bull whip and was a crack rifle shooter. California Joe was the trainer and stage handler of Pinto, and an expert plain and fancy trick roper.

Working together, Frank, Joe, and Pinto put on a fascinating show. Their stage names overshadowed their family name, which I have since forgotten. They lived in Canada and toured as a family during the summer accompanied by Joe's wife, who was Frank's daughter, and their young child.

Montana Frank —Pinto— California Joe

From mid-morning until show time, the family spent each day at the barn with me. During those weeks we became close friends. That is when the stage show, "Smilin' Bill" and his Wonder Horse "King," was created and fashioned.

When Joe realized how serious I was about entertaining, he offered to teach me how to train King to perform on stage like his horse Pinto. I jumped at the chance to learn those skills and devoted my spare time to perfecting them.

During that time together I received detailed lessons from California Joe on how to train King for the stage, and instructions for plain trick roping. Frank taught me how to handle the Australian bull whip. I was in cowboy heaven.

Chapter 9 California Joe, King, and Me

King was a gifted horse with a gentle disposition. His strength required special handling on my part as we worked together perfecting our show. He was also a proud stallion who thoroughly enjoyed servicing all the mares brought to him for breeding.

The secret to horsemanship is to never let your horse know he is stronger than you. Knowing this, I always maintained control, never allowing King to entertain the idea that he was bigger and stronger. I handled him gently and King returned the favor.

The hardest part of training a horse to perform on stage is hiding the cues from the audience while communicating with the horse. The crowd wants to be entertained by the mystery of a horse that can seemingly talk to them on his own.

To accomplish that mystery requires the sleight of hand and disarming slyness of a good magician, as well as the skills of a good trainer.

Prayer Time; Playing Dead

King learned to say "Yes" by nodding his head up and down and "No" by shaking it. Then he learned to count by pawing with his left front leg. All my cues occurred from his left except when laying down.

The signals were given by shifting my body and hands while holding a short riding crop. The signal for "Yes" was my best secret. It occurred without any body movement or even the blinking of my eye.

These tricks were followed with King kneeling on his front knees in several positions. Eventually, I lay him completely over onto his left side with his head laying flat on the ground.

In the first chapter of this book, "Onstage with Bill and King," you will find a description of King's many stage tricks and most of our secret commands.

King and I had only one serious riding accident.

It happened when we were promoting the ranch one holiday by riding through the resort area. King was dressed in his best bridle and saddle and I was also smartly dressed.

Before the Galloping Somersault

Chapter 9 California Joe, King, and Me

Beatley's Hotel

We passed Beatley's Hotel and cantered slowly on a narrow street over the bridge to Orchard Island. On the downward slope of the street, King stumbled. His front legs buckled, causing a galloping head-first somersault onto the hard pavement.

It happened in an instant, although it seemed like slow motion. Thanks to instincts I learned while riding bareback, I leaned away from the direction of his fall as his hind quarters flew past my head.

King was a large horse and landed on his face, neck, shoulders, and back before sliding to a stop and rolling onto his left side. I stayed astride King inside of the somersault and landed on my side with my left leg caught beneath the saddle and King.

I remember we both lay very quietly for several seconds before attempting to get up. We were both dazed as we slowly clambered to our feet and studied each other. I could see concern in King's eyes, but no fear. Neither of us was frightened, but we both felt embarrassed.

His face, knees, shoulders, and back were bloody against the golden color of his coat. My pants were ripped and one pant leg was nearly torn off. The bridle and saddle were ripped and scarred from bearing King's weight as he skidded to a stop on the pavement. We were both a mess, but we were both in one piece, with all our parts intact.

I was thankful that nothing was broken as we slowly made our way back to the stable about a mile away. While healing, we shared each other's pain and grew even closer.

Even the thought of a running horse turning a somersault brings alarm to both horse and rider. I'm sure many riders have shared similar falls with their horse companions. Hopefully, they were as fortunate as King and I were on that day.

Chapter Ten

A SPINNING ROPE SEEMS TO FLOAT

As a youngster I played with ropes around the farm. I made my first spinning rope from Mom's clothes line. Later on, like a sailor on his ship, I fiddled with ropes in my slow time at the ranch. However, all my attempts at doing rope tricks failed miserably.

I was amazed the first time I saw California Joe perform rope tricks and asked him to teach me. He was an expert at plain and fancy trick roping and could wow an audience with his polished routine.

Joe instructed me to acquire a 3/8 inch cotton rope about 25 feet long and make a Honda on one end. To do that, he said to double the end back about 2½ inches to make the Honda, and fasten it with lightweight copper wire wrapped with black tape.

Then I made a loop by slipping the opposite end of the rope through the Honda. My first attempt at spinning bombed badly and the loop twisted into a knot. Looking on and smiling, California Joe said, "Bill, let me show you how it's done."

"Here's the secret," he said, as he coiled the rope onto my left hand with my palm up. He made sure

The Honda

the coils would drop off my fingers as they were drawn into the loop. Then he shook out a loop until it hung down half my height and placed it in my right hand

I eliminated the kinks by unwinding the rope. When the loop was completely open, I moved the Honda forward to make a spoke for the loop. Joe explained the wheel-and-spoke principle where my right hand was the hub and the loop was the wheel.

I held the three-foot-long hanging loop in my right hand with palm down. He placed the spoke between my thumb and last two fingers. Then he curled my first two fingers under the loop rope.

Joe said, "To start the spin hold the rope lightly in your hand and let the loop slip from your fingers as you cast your right hand in a counter-clockwise horizontal circle. Then let the centrifugal spin-

The Light Grip

Chapter 10 A Spinning Rope Seems to Float

ning forces hold the rope in the air."

As I did, the loop seemed to float in the air all by itself. "WOW," I said. "I really can do this. It's fun."

My hand moved faster and the rope became more alive as the flat loop grew into a larger circle. As it opened out larger, my confidence grew stronger and a big smile covered my face. I finally let the loop fall to the ground. Success!!

But wait a minute! The next attempt was a total disaster. I had forgotten the directions and the rope kinked into a big knot. I asked Joe to show me again how to shake out the kinks and hold the rope.

Start of the Flat Loop Spin

This time I studied the light grip of the rope in my hands for a minute before attempting to cast the rope from my fingers. It was another success.

That was only the beginning lesson. As soon as I mastered one trick, Joe would show me another. Joe was a great teacher who could spin a rope in each hand at the same time. His ropes moved magically through the air in a flawless routine.

Bill Jumps into the Loop at Cowboy Town

The Vertical Loop Goes Up and Over the Head

Chapter 10 A Spinning Rope Seems to Float

The Body Loop at the Ranch

I decided to master only those routines I needed for the show, and even those took hours and hours of practice. After mastering the flat loop, I learned how to jump inside and then turn it into a full body loop.

Holding the coil of rope in my left hand, I spun a flat loop. When the spoke of the loop was in exactly the right position, I jumped inside the loop with both feet. My right hand shot up above my head to keep the rope spinning as I dropped the coil from my left hand to eliminate kinking.

Then Joe taught me the vertical loop and how to move it up and over my head into a full body loop. Normally performed with a 25-foot rope, it took little effort and onlookers would join me inside the loop.

Body Loop while Standing on King's Side

When I stepped up onto King's side during the stage show and filled the stage with my larger 50-foot loop, the audience would gasp in amazement.

Another great trick is the butterfly spin, which is sometimes called the reverse spin. In this maneuver, a small vertical-like spin is started on the left side of the waist. After two spins, it is reversed by moving the wrist to the right side and revolving the loop in the opposite direction.

The action is reversed after two spins on each side of the body. The butterfly spin can be brought into a vertical spin and moved up over the head into a body spin. This is a good-looking routine.

Joe also taught me a couple of half-hitch tricks that involved the audience. These tricks require a 25-foot spinning rope and an unsuspecting volunteer.

To perform the overhead half-hitch, I snug the rope around the volunteer's shoulders. Holding the lead rope slightly taunt in my hand, I step back to the end of the rope and coil an 18-inch loop under the lead rope with my right hand.

Chapter 10 A Spinning Rope Seems to Float

The Overhead Half-Hitch by Bill during a Show at Cowboy Town near Nashville, Tennessee

After placing the loop gingerly on top of my right shoulder, I flip the lead rope high in the air with my left hand and forcefully cast the small loop forward in a large counterclockwise snap of my right wrist while throwing my arm forward.

This creates a large loop that travels under the lead rope. Guided by the lead rope, it sails over the head and settles down around the volunteer's body.

When finished, my roping partner is tied up from head to foot. Each half-hitch rope loop must then be removed separately from around the partner, who is usually quite relieved to be free again.

If the procedure is reversed, the same trick can be performed by throwing flat half-hitches under the feet of the partner. First I snug a loop around the partner's waist and then step back, letting the lead rope lay slightly taut on the ground.

Overhead Half-Hitch in the Bahama Islands

Facing the partner with the end of the lead rope in my right hand, I quickly step forward with my left leg while leaning forward and thrusting the rope in a large counterclockwise loop.

When the loop reaches the half way spot, I tell the partner to jump high with both feet. By timing it right, the loop passes under the feet during the jump and travels up around the legs and waist. The flat loops continue until the partner is completely tied. This trick always pleases those who are watching.

Trick roping has become my signature event at book-signings and speaking engagements. When the host introduces me as an award-winning author, book publisher, engineer, and cowboy entertainer, I step forward, dressed in a business suit and red tie.

Chapter 10 A Spinning Rope Seems to Float

I begin by saying, "It's true! I've had many successful careers. However, it's hard to believe you are looking at a professional cowboy entertainer and trick roper when I'm dressed in a dark suit and tie."

"I grew up with big cowboy dreams on a farm in Ohio. Before the age of 18, I was singing on the radio and headlining a Western stage show called 'Smilin' Bill and his Wonder Horse King'."

With that, I open my briefcase and pull out an ugly brown kinky rope, saying, "I picked this rope up in a barnyard to show you that my rope spinning is real. If you can spin this type of rope you

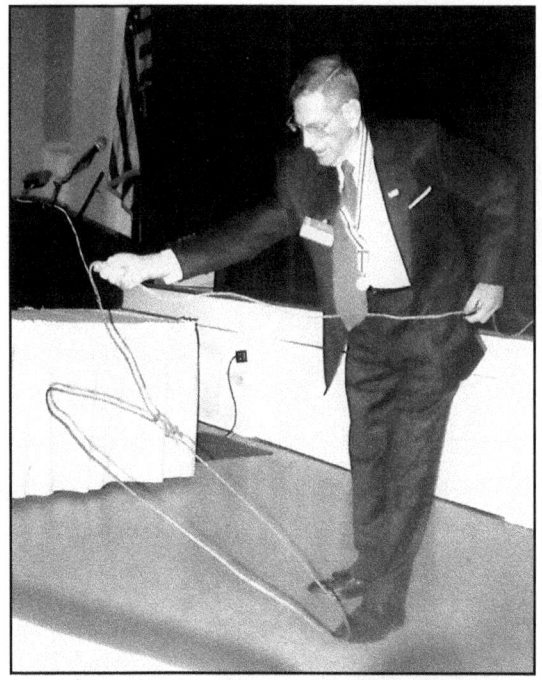

Bill Performing Rope Trick at SAR Luncheon in Daytona Beach, Florida

can spin almost anything. It's a skill you never forget."

I explain how important it is to first remove the kinks. Then I carefully lay the rope onto my palms and fingers, bend slightly forward, and quickly spin it into a flat loop before jumping inside.

When the room ceiling is high, I may spin the rope into a vertical loop and then move it up and over my head into a body loop. When I drop the rope to the floor the skeptics in the audience applaud.

They may not remember what I say, but they never forget the rope tricks.

Chapter Eleven

DIAMOND J RANCH ROAD SHOW

As I mentioned earlier, Lew Jenkins worked for the U.S. Postal Service as a rural mail route carrier. I didn't mention, however, that Lew was also a very skilled rider and horseman. Our love of horses led us to develop very similar riding and training styles.

As a sideline to his postal work, Lew owned and operated the Diamond J Ranch and riding stable in the resort area of Russells Point, Ohio. Located along the southern banks of Indian Lake, the ranch was home to the stable of horses Lew rented to visitors vacationing in the resort area.

Lew's children, Ralph and Donna, were not much older than me. Although Lew was aware that they had little interest in his horses, he did not let that stop him from pursuing his dreams. When King and I were ready to perform on stage, Lew decided to organize a Western road show

The following newspaper clipping, entitled "Road Show Being Organized," was published on December 21, 1951 in the *Bellefontaine Examiner*, which serves Logan County, Ohio, and surrounding areas.

Road Show Being Organized

Chapter 11 Diamond J Ranch Road Show

Believed to be the first western show ever to emanate from Logan county is the Diamond J Ranch Round-up that will make its debut at Bluffton, Ind., Saturday night, Dec. 29.

It is being organized and directed by Lew Jenkins, Lewistown mail carrier, who has carved a niche in the entertainment world with his donkey basketball and baseball features, and his celebrated Palomino, King, a golden stallion, which has been exhibited by Johnny Mack Brown, well-known western film actor, although the trained animal is owned by Mr. Jenkins.

The Logan countian has built a two-hour show that features the comical basketball game, several vaudeville acts and music by the popular Diamond J Ranch Hands under the supervision of "Smiling" Bill Cummins. They are all Logan countians. In the above photo they are; back row, left to right, Norman Williams, Lowell "Doc" Crock, Charles Woodell. In the front row, left to right, are Perry Price, Johnny Green and Bill Cummins, all exponents of western and hill billy music.

In the cast, too, are Montana Frank and California Joe, a brace of entertainers. The latter is the MC of the show and is also an expert at rope spinning, plain and fancy.

Montana Frank, a master of the Australian bull whip, exhibits El Toro, an 800-pound Hereford bull trained in many ways.

King, the Palomino mentioned above, is sent through his paces by Mr. Cummins and the stunts include the camel stretch, Arab prayer, salute with striking hoof, curtsies, cake walk, and he even answers questions by the nod of his head.

Besides King there is Jimmy, the roller skating horse owned and trained by Albert McAlexander of Kiser Lake. Jimmy is a young Pinto and he and his master are fairly new in the show business although they have appeared publicly on several occasions.

The various acts are sandwiched in between the quarters of the donkey basketball game. At the present time Mr. Jenkins has two donkey troupes on the road. One is handled by John Cummins and the other by Ray Wilcox. They reside in Lewistown and Russells Point, respectively, and already this season have conducted nearly 50 games in Ohio and surrounding states.

I had forgotten about the article until it was given to me by a friend 50 years later, while I was attending the funeral of my Dad's sister in Ohio. I tucked it away with my cowboy photographs, never realizing its importance in the writing of this book.

The top picture in the clipping is King and me during Prayer Time. It was taken on stage during our show in the majestic Holland Theatre in Bellefontaine. The photograph on the front cover of this book was taken outside before that show began.

To provide background music for the road show, I assembled a country and Western band known as the Diamond J Ranch Hands. All the members were extremely talented and, like me, played their music by ear. A picture of our band was highlighted in the newspaper article mentioned above.

The band member's names in the first clipping from left to right in the back row are Norman Williams, Lowell "Doc" Crock, and Charles Woodell. In the front row, from left to right, are Perry Price, Johnny Green, and me, Bill Cummins.

In the cast were Montana Frank and California Joe. Our show was emceed by Joe who performed amazing plain and fancy rope spinning. They also traveled with their own Western stage show.

Montana Frank entertained the crowd with his 800 pound Hereford bull, El Toro. Stage trained in many ways, El Toro added realism to Frank's skills with the rifle, and his mastery of the Australian bull whip cracking through the air.

Chapter 11 Diamond J Ranch Road Show

Montana Frank; California Joe

Lew Jenkins also owned two donkey ball teams. One was handled by my cousin, John Cummins, and the other by Ray Wilcox. Each donkey team traveled in a converted school bus as they entertained crowds throughout the Midwest.

Donkey ball is still popular today. It is played on the ball field or in the basketball gymnasium. Two teams of players are chosen from local communities to ride the donkeys. The donkey handlers

One of the Diamond J Ranch Donkey Ball Teams

Lew & John Cummins; Two-Gun Bill

referee the one and a half hour game with their whistles.

Players can either ride or lead their donkey but must be mounted to move the ball. Spectators are delighted as donkeys do their thing and frustrate the riders. It doesn't matter how well you can ride, your donkey will cause you embarrassment as you play.

Besides King, there was Jimmy the roller-skating horse. He was owned and trained by Albert McAlexander of nearby Kiser Lake. They were fairly new to the show but had appeared publicly on many occasions. The sight of a horse on roller skates just wowed the audience.

Chapter 11 Diamond J Ranch Road Show

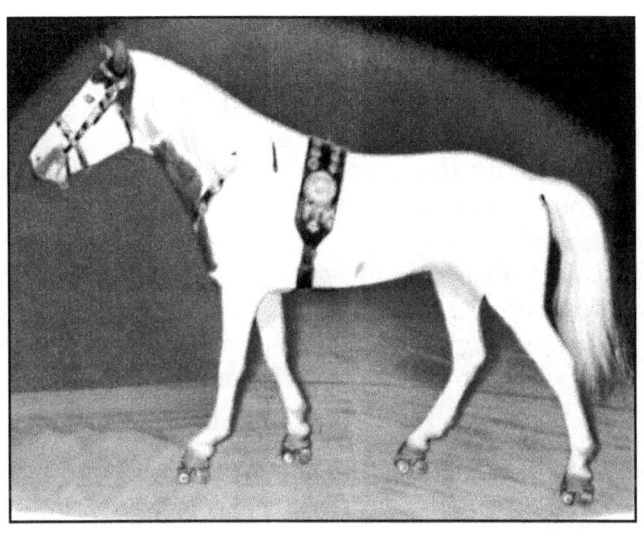

Jimmy the Roller-skating Horse; and with Albert McAlexander, his Owner and Trainer

It excites me that no matter how much machinery replaces the horse, the work it can do is still measured in horsepower...even in this space age. And although a riding horse often weighs half a ton, and a big drafter a full ton, either can be led about by a piece of string if he has been wisely trained. This to me is a constant source of wonder, and challenge.

Marguerite Henry

Chapter Twelve

DITCH THE PSYCHIATRIST COUCH

All I pay my psychiatrist is the cost of feed and hay and he'll listen to me any day.
Author Unknown

Have you noticed that with the departure of the horse came the proliferation of psychoanalysts around the world? Thinking logically then, the psychiatrist couch has become a substitute for the companionship of mankind's best friend.

And no, I don't mean the dog or cat. Mankind's best friend is the horse! Then let us consider this: time with a horse is great therapy for the soul.

With the horse, we have a big, warm animal to talk to who will listen but will not talk back. With proper care, it does not get angry and with proper handling, it shows no aggressive tendencies.

Perhaps you have noticed that psychiatrists have these same traits. Like the horse, they listen without anger or aggressiveness. But unlike the horse, they charge huge sums of money to hear you share your thoughts while on their soft comfortable couches.

Do they both work? Yes, they do!

But there is a very big difference. A good horse will actually feel and share your pain. Ten minutes with a horse is worth more that 100 hours on the doctor's couch. By using the same technique as the psychiatrist, they can actually help you solve your problems.

Emotional mending happens to us while caring for and riding a horse. Riding horses gives children and adults with mental, physical, and emotional challenges both strength and independence. A horse, then, in reality, becomes a source of identity for the rider.

The horse provides an activity the rider quickly learns to love. Riding is not just for pleasure, but for mental and physical therapy. This sense of identity with a particular horse becomes the highlight of the week, and soon turns into one of the most important aspects of therapeutic riding.

Through their eyes, ears, and touch, the horse and rider can sense the state of being of one another. I believe there truly is something special about this unique relationship. It is as if both horse and rider were created with the uncanny ability to commune with each other.

This exchange must take place at the heart and head levels to be permanent. The interaction of heart and head can occur from being to being which is why a horse makes us feel at one with him.

When the horse becomes a messenger to our own well being, it begins to lower our blood pressure and stress level.

Unlike any other pet, the mere size of a horse becomes a challenge. Taking control of this living creature as we ride, changes the way we feel about ourselves. With the reins we can guide the animal in any direction, and with our voice we can control its movements. Embracing this power changes us and imbues us with self esteem.

Feeling better is a subtle change at first, which is why we return, again and again, to ride. As we gain more and more confidence in handling our horse, we take more control of our life.

Led by a Young Girl with Rope (Photo by Tara H. O'Gorman)

A word of caution here! During my lifetime, high-tech gadgetry has taken over much of our lives in this country. We watch a television or a computer

The Ranch Visitors Loved to Pose with King

screen instead of reading books or working with our hands making things.

These changes may require our brain to function and process information differently. Only time will reveal what kind of impact this uncharted water will thrust upon future generations.

Could it be possible that acquiring some good old fashioned "horse sense" gives us more control over our lives? Can horse therapy help us avoid the need for a psychiatrist's couch?

You be the judge. Based upon my experiences, I believe introducing "horse sense" back into our lives will enrich it. There is something long lasting about this man/horse relationship that warrants taking the time to experience and appreciate it.

Chapter Thirteen

COWBOYS DO NOT PULL LEATHER

*Riding, like every other bodily exercise,
does not feel like what it looks like.*

Author Unknown

When I taught guests at the ranch how to ride, they were only allowed to hold onto the saddle horn until the stirrups were adjusted and they knew how to start, stop, and turn their horse. I explained, "Only a 'tenderfoot' rider is allowed to hold on to the saddle horn to keep from falling off."

I taught them to hold both reins in one hand and to keep both hands in the air above the saddle horn while riding, so they would not confuse their horse. I further explained that, "A confused horse is easily spooked which is why real cowboys would rather fall off than pull leather."

To someone who has never ridden a horse, this may sound reckless. Believe me, it isn't. If you don't learn to properly sit on a horse the first time you ride, you can get hurt. While running the ranch, I taught hundreds of tenderfoot riders how to ride safely without anyone hurting themselves.

I never had a problem teaching those new riders because I matched them to the proper horse from the stable. The riding trail made a large loop around the level pasture behind the stable, so I could keep an eye on everything. Every rider rode clockwise around the trail, and there were no exceptions. The new riders were safe because the horses could be trusted.

I taught the more serious riders differently than I taught tenderfoot riders at the ranch. To protect the guest riders, I mounted them on a saddle first. I would never do that to someone wanting to become a serious rider.

Some said I was a natural horseman and maybe that was true. But perhaps it only seemed to be true because I had learned to ride properly while riding bareback. The only way to get the feel of the horse under you in all situations is by riding bareback. To be a great rider you must learn to ride without a saddle.

Learning to ride in a saddle first will reduce your riding skills for the rest of your life. Your enjoyment will also be hampered permanently. You are like a baby chick that is weakened if it is helped out of its egg shell. Don't let anyone talk you out of it. Hold your ground and find a different teacher if you must.

To be a great rider, you must learn to become one with the horse. The horse does not and cannot take the initiative to become one with its rider. The horse can only become what you teach it. Its sole desire is to please its rider.

In other words, much like the alpha dog in a canine situation, if you do not take control and behave as if you are in charge, then the horse will be confused.

Riding bareback will not only teach balance, but will also teach leg control. The horse can only do what it does naturally while taking guidance from the rider. After all, the horse is doing all the heavy lifting while, at the same time, interpreting the rider's signals.

A well trained horse places all its trust in the hands of the rider. If you tell it to run full speed over a cliff, it will do so. Its whole reactive process is geared to fulfilling the latest command from the rider, so the rider had better know what he wants the horse to do next. If not, there is trouble brewing.

Mixed signals will confuse the horse and cause it to resort to its own senses. Unlocking itself from the rider and looking ahead, it will react instinctively to any danger that may come up. Out of fear, it may run away or turn from the trail and return to the stable. And it may, for the first time, realize that it is actually stronger than the rider. Very dangerous!

It is very dangerous for the rider and anyone else who gets in the way. The horse will run straight through a crowd of people, or even worse, into the path of a speeding vehicle. When fear is driving the horse, anything can happen and usually does.

Learning to ride bareback will teach you the skills you need to control your horse, which protects both of you. Let us take a look at what you should learn while riding bareback.

It starts with balance. God designed the rider's bottom and the horse's back to blend together. When you grip the sides of the horse tightly with your legs, it soon becomes natural to you and to the horse. After all, it's skin against skin, so the nerves of both can react quickly to changing conditions.

While riding bareback, you can teach the horse many leg and body signals. You touch the horse lightly with both legs to move forward and with one leg at a time to turn or to move sideways.

Accompany these actions with voice and rein signals as well, for an even better response. It is amazing how quickly you will feel comfortable on the horse.

One of the most important lessons learned while riding bareback is how to fall off without

King and Bill in a Parade Stretch

hurting yourself. Don't worry about falling! After all, you are not very far above the ground when riding. When done correctly, you will find your horse waiting for you to get back up and remount.

You may be surprised that I believe you need to learn how to fall off your horse. Think about it. You teach kids how to fall safely when they are learning to ride a bike and to skate. Coping with falling is a very important aspect of every physical activity.

Always ride with both reins untied and held in one hand a few inches above the horse's neck. This, of course, means riding a horse trained with Western style neck reining. When you fall, you can hold onto one rein and stop your horse. You should never let go of the rein from the side you fall.

This leads to a very important point that was mentioned before, but bears repeating.

Cowboys do not pull leather.

The cowboys I've known would rather fall off than be seen holding on to the saddle horn. Grown men and women who grab the saddle horn while riding make me want to shout out "greenhorn" and "tenderfoot" and look away in shame.

Such riders are adults behaving like children. A rider who cannot stay on his horse without pulling leather should let someone who can handle the horse take his place. I hope cowboy dignity will return.

The only time a cowboy should grab the saddle horn while riding is to mount and dismount. I've ridden thousands of miles and never held onto the horn except during trick riding.

A few times when my arms were tired I have rested my hand on top of the saddle horn. I always turned my palm upward. It was absolutely critical that no one thought I was holding on to the horn.

Professional speakers are taught early in their careers not to touch anything while speaking. If at all possible, they will not hold onto the podium, the lectern, notes, or anything else while talking. They know that doing so drains their energy into the object they touch, and their message loses power.

The same thing happens when a rider grabs the saddle horn. His energy drains into the saddle and forces the horse to maintain the rider's balance as well as its own. This is unfair to both horse and rider and should be stopped.

Pulling leather is not a problem when new riders learn to ride bareback without the aid of a saddle. "Barebacking" is the secret because the things you learn while riding bareback can be transferred later to a saddle ride. The horse will know immediately what you are thinking and will react accordingly.

Remember this key. A good rider lets his horse feel what he wants through the seat of his pants and the feel of his legs. Don't skip this vital lesson as you learn to ride. Become a competent rider and do it correctly.

Properly trained, a cowboy can be a horse's best friend.
                                        William A. Cummins

Chapter Fourteen

300 MILES ON HORSEBACK

We closed the riding stable on Labor Day. I was 18 years old when the summer tourist season ended at the Diamond J Ranch. Early the next morning I said, "Dad, I'll be away for a couple of weeks. I'm going on a horseback trip to Aurora, Illinois."

He didn't look too surprised, but he asked, "Why are you going to do that?" I had been anticipating his question and quickly replied, "Because I'll probably never get another chance."

I watched as Dad slowly remembered some of his own youthful escapades. Then he smiled and never asked another question about the trip. Needless to say, I was right, because I have never been asked to do it again. Chances are pretty good that I never will.

The trip idea came up when an insurance man from Aurora, Illinois, visited our ranch and riding stable. He and his girlfriend were vacationing in the Russells Point Resort near the end of the summer season and both rode nearly every day at the ranch.

He was an experienced rider, so Lew let him ride our best stable horse, Lady, the high-spirited mare that only Lew and I could safely ride. She was Lew's favorite horse other than King. The insurance man liked her, and I knew why.

Lady was a tall sorrel mare with an easy ride. The movements of her body and legs were soft and gentle. You felt like you were sitting in an easy chair when on Lady's back.

Insurance Man Holding the Horses He Bought

The insurance man offered to buy her, and Lew reluctantly agreed. I cannot recall the man's name, but he also bought a horse for his girlfriend from Bob Kennedy, who was boarding his horse at the stable. While visiting the ranch, the insurance man saw how much Bob and I liked to ride every day.

After the sale we discussed transportation of the horses. He said, "Bill, if you and Bob want to ride the horses to my home, I'll pay your trip expenses there and back." Without hesitation, we both jumped at his offer. Thus began our 300 miles journey to his home in Illinois.

Chapter 14 300 Miles on Horseback

Neither Bob nor I had much money, so he gave us $100 for our travel expenses during the trip. We had no camping utensils or sleeping bags, so we decided to rough it like the old time cowboys by sleeping out under the stars on the horse's saddle blankets using the saddles for our pillows.

A Normal Day at the Ranch for Bill and Bob

Our plan was to buy or borrow grain and water for the horses from local farmers as we traveled. If the weather turned rainy or cold, we would ask permission to stay in their barns. We would buy our own food at local stores as we rode along the way.

Being young and naive, Bob and I really didn't anticipate any other problems or needs. We only spent a couple of days envisioning our needs and then gathered things together for one of the most memorable experiences of our lives. Looking back, I really believe God watches over cowboys.

Early one morning we began our amazing eight day odyssey. Bob and I wrapped a change of clothing in an old army blanket and tied it to the back of our saddles, secured our lariats, mounted up, and left the stable, heading west toward Indiana.

We Saddled Up and Away We Rode

Dressed in well-worn high-heeled cowboy boots, Levis, cotton shirts, and wide-brimmed hats, we looked the part of old time trail riders as we began our trip to Aurora.

We made our way a few miles north along US Route 33 from Russells Point, Ohio to the small town of New Hampshire where the route turned west toward Wapakoneta and St. Marys, Ohio. We spent the first night in a small clump of trees along the highway near St. Marys.

After hobbling the horses, we bedded down on the grassy ground. We stretched out on the blankets with our heads on the saddles and our hats pulled down over our faces. Needless to say, the ground was uncomfortable for boys who were not accustomed to it, but we toughed it out, cowboy style.

We rose early and eased our aching bodies back into the saddle, then continued our way along US Route 33. The highway turned northwest where we hoped to find a warm barn to stay in the next night.

Chapter 14 300 Miles on Horseback

As luck would have it, we happened upon a livestock sale barn as we approached Decatur, Indiana. We enjoyed sleeping inside the barn because the nights were already turning cooler.

Bedded Down for the Night

Heading out early the next day, we continued northwest along US Route 33 toward Fort Wayne, Indiana. As we neared the city, I noticed my horse, Lady, was losing one of her rubber insulated shoes. After inquiry of the local farmers, we were directed to a blacksmith who could replace Lady's shoe.

While waiting for the shoe replacement, someone notified the Fort Wayne newspaper about a couple of cowboys passing through. The reporter arrived just before we left, asked us a lot of questions, and took our pictures which appeared in their paper the next day. Sadly, I have lost my copy of the article but I hope to retrieve another copy of it someday.

From Fort Wayne we turned west and rode in the median of multilane US Route 30 all the way to

Aurora, Illinois. During most nights on the trip, we boarded our horses and slept in farmer's barns.

One night we walked into town, rented a motel room, took a shower, and got a good night's rest. As fate would have it, during the next night we suffered through one of the coldest experiences of our lives.

Usually, we rode about 10 hours each day and traveled between 35 and 40 miles. Bob and I were quiet most of the time because we had run out of things to talk about.

Without paying attention, the day ended and night closed in on us. By the time we thought about looking for a farm where we could bed down, it was too late. This left us no choice but to keep riding all night.

A cold front set in, and it was just about midnight when we slipped on our extra clothes. Large tractor trailers roared past us all night. Each one sent an ice cold wind ripping around both horse and rider. It whipped our clothes, causing us to shudder as each rig sped by.

By 3:00 A.M., we were off our horses and walking with our army blankets wrapped around us to keep warm. We were both silent, too cold to speak.

Never has a morning sunrise been so welcome. It warmed our backs as we walked slowly while leading our horses along the multilane highway. The horses had grown as weary as Bob and I and were not happy when we mounted up again.

We spotted a farm house with a small horse barn after a couple of hours riding. Leaving the highway, we headed down the country road and up a lane to where some children were playing.

After hearing our freezing all-nighter story, the lady of the house invited us to stable and feed our horses and rest awhile. It looked like rain and began to sprinkle, so we quickly accepted her invitation.

The skies cleared, and we decided to keep riding after eating and resting a couple of hours. When I threw the saddle on Lady, she rolled her eyes and glared at me. As I cinched it tight, she stomped her front feet and let out a snort.

I could tell she wasn't happy, but we mounted up and said our goodbyes. By the time we headed out the lane, Lady was downright mad. We crossed the road in front of the house and turned left onto the grassy roadside berm.

Lady took about ten steps, stopped, dropped to her knees, and lay down with me still in the saddle. I straddled her body with my legs as she lay down, wondering if she was sick.

Then I realized she was only pouting. She was having a horsey fit and pulling a "sit down strike." It took a bit of horse diplomacy to get her back onto her feet. That means I kicked her in the rump with my boot.

Lady showed her displeasure all day long as we continued our trek westward. She had learned her lesson, and Bob and I learned a lesson as well.

We never made the mistake of ignoring the time again or neglecting to make preparations for staying overnight. We began looking early for a place to stay.

Taking a Midday Rest Break

During the last day of our trek, we rode mostly through urban communities south of Chicago. The most dangerous part of the trip was leading our horses over a long open grated bridge near the city of Joliet, Illinois.

The horses grew ever more fearful as the ground mysteriously disappeared from under them and they could see nothing below their feet. We moved with great care to keep the shoes on their small hooves from slipping through the grating surface.

Lucky for us, they followed faithfully across to solid ground as the cars and trucks kept whizzing past us. I'm still amazed at the enormous trust my 1,000 pound horse put into a 150-pound teenage boy. I'm sure Bob felt the same way about his horse.

We rode a few more miles before stopping at a phone and calling the owner of the horses. He sent

Chapter 14 300 Miles on Horseback

a horse van to pick us up and take us the remaining distance through the busy city streets.

The horses seemed relieved when Bob and I finally turned them out to pasture and said goodbye. We were very proud indeed of our faithful steeds.

The owner invited us to stay over a few days, but only on one condition. We had to agree to bathe and wash our clothes right away. Our horsey trail aroma could not be tolerated any longer.

We were happy to agree and turned ourselves over to the blessings of hot water and soapy suds. Our trek was successful; our job was finished. We delivered his horses safe and sound as promised.

A couple of days later we started making plans to head back home to Ohio. We decided to travel by bus since it stopped near our homes. The owner obliged and dropped us off at the Greyhound Bus terminal along with our saddles and tack.

We were an unusual sight to most city folk. As we strode by in high heeled cowboy boots, we could see the kids tug eagerly at their parent's sleeves. We looked out of place in cowboy outfits, carrying our saddles over our shoulders with our saddle blankets tucked under our arms.

I must say we liked all the attention and walked with a little swagger knowing we had successfully completed a 300 mile trip on horseback. All things considered, it was quite an accomplishment.

Neither Bob nor I realized at the time just how special our trip would become. Riding 300 miles on horseback through modern traffic in eight days has become even more unique with the passing of time

Six decades have passed, and I have never heard of any other cowboy having such a great experience. I was blessed indeed, and I am eternally grateful.

The irony of it all was that I picked up a terrible head cold and bad cough while traveling back home. Seems I was safer on the open road with a faithful horse under me than in a modern Greyhound Bus.

Life is good when you are astride a horse.

Chapter Fifteen

JUST CALL IT HORSE SENSE

I grew up watching my Dad train his horses for work on the farm. He was an excellent horseman who had learned from his father and grandfather. My farming heritage goes back through Ireland into Scotland in the sixteenth century and beyond that into Europe.

Dad's cardinal rule for handling horses was this, "If you make your horse mind when it is in the barn, it will mind when it is out of the barn." To use this rule, teach your horse only one idea at a time. If you try to do more, both you and the horse will come away with nothing. (This works with children, too.)

By observing Dad closely, I discovered there are four basic steps you should follow in this order to teach and train almost any horse:

1. Get acquainted
2. Take charge
3. Establish trust
4. Give reward

Based upon this understanding, you must give your horse a lot of personal attention, and if your horse is to achieve its true potential, you can never treat your horse as a playmate.

It is critical also that you understood three basic facts about horses. To successfully train your horse you must learn them well:

- Horses have a natural desire to be friendly
- Horses cannot reason — they can only react
- All their learning will be self-taught

You must be trustworthy and willing to interact personally by talking to your horse constantly. You must give it freedom and guidance simultaneously. You must praise it, and you must also occasionally correct it.

To make your horse grow ever more trustful and dependable, you must understand that your job as the handler will never go away. If you will not or cannot do these things, then forget the idea of ever entering it into competition or taking it on stage.

Always try to train your horse when he is rested. Any distraction can keep him from focusing on what you are trying to accomplish. Also, you must approve the action he just performed for you by immediately providing positive feedback.

The ideal method of feedback is with your voice along with patting and stroking. If your horse trusts and likes you, he will always want to please you. You rarely give food as a reward because he does not need it. In other words, your horse will work hard and work smart simply to please you.

As you can see in the following pictures, King is concentrating on following my commands.

Sitting — Ears Back

Parade Stretch — A Good Picture Pose

 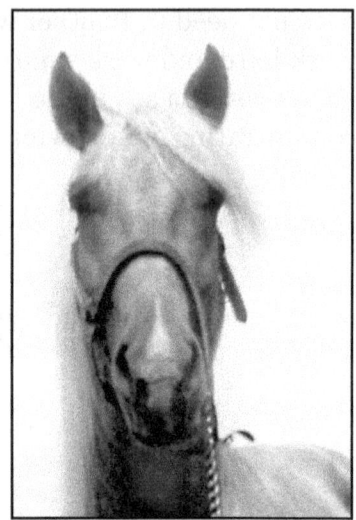

Ears Back and Forward, Listening for My Voice

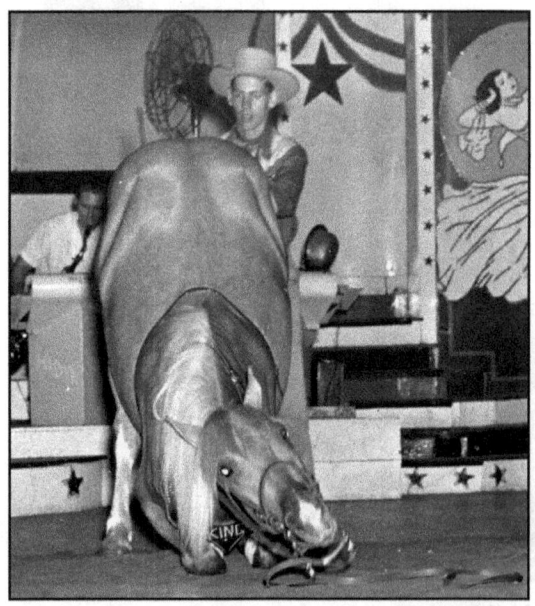

*The Camel Stretch with King's
Head Cocked to See Me*

Chapter 15 Just Call It Horse Sense

I truly believe what actually motivated King was his innate desire to please me. In his genes, he felt personal pride and gratification when I rewarded him for a job well done. When you study his ears, eyes, and skin, you can see this was true.

As the trainer, you must begin to take charge the very instant you meet. As soon as the horse senses you are serious, it will try to communicate. You must never forget that a horse can react to you but cannot reason. With this knowledge you can teach it to trust you with its very life, but never fear you.

Don't waste time trying to teach your horse how a train makes a loud whistle sound. He will never figure it out. Instead, concentrate on teaching him to trust and obey you. A properly trained horse will follow you almost anywhere.

If you do not understand these things, focus on your riding skills and leave the training of the horse to a professional. Skilled horsemen know that any kind of so-called horse sense is simply another way of saying common sense.

There are a few more things to understand when working with horses. A horse doesn't transfer what it sees with one eye to the other eye. This means it must be given the same training on both sides to be fully trusted.

For instance, if you saddle up and mount from only the left side, the horse will not be comfortable if you switch sides. The Indians in the west mounted from the right side. Many cowboys were surprised when they tried to mount an Indian's pony.

The horse uses its nose to touch objects instead of smelling them. Sometimes they will snort as they do this, thus giving the impression of trying to smell the object. They only want to touch it. You should give them plenty of time to satisfy their curiosity.

When a horse lies down, it drops first to its front knees and then rolls over onto its side. It gets up by lifting itself onto its front legs and then swivels its hind legs beneath its body to stand up.

As a horse eats grass, it chops the grass with its upper teeth by tilting its head downward. It is also fun to let a horse eat from your hand. Their lips are able to nibble gently as they lift the treat into their mouth. This is a child's delight and brings laughter.

The hair of a horse slopes down and backwards from front to rear. They will naturally face into the wind and can easily be ridden into the wind during a storm. This is important when riding the range.

Horses do not eat meat, but are herbivores, living on grains and grass. In the wild, the mares run in herds under a stallion's protection.

Horses are indeed fascinating to watch as they move about. I'm deeply grateful they are our friends, and truly believe God created them for humans to use and enjoy.

Through industrial history we have honored the horse by measuring work in horsepower. We even compare our automobiles by how many horsepower they can produce. I believe this is a lasting tribute to this most noble creature.

Chapter Sixteen

A SIMPLE LESSON IN TRUST

A tamed horse can never be made wild again.
                    William A. Cummins

Not every horse is teachable. My Dad said, "If the horse doesn't have any space between its ears, forget it." You can learn a horse's personality by studying the shape of its head and its eyes. Study it, and always watch the ears. King had the ideal horse's head.

Working with a new horse requires getting to know and trust each other. I focused solely on the horse and my mission. I was never in a hurry when working with horses and did not allow a lot of distraction to go on around me. I began with the horse free in a small fenced enclosure about 25 feet square.

When I stepped inside the enclosure and closed the gate, the lesson began. As I talked quietly to the horse, it would react naturally by turning away from me. With legs nervously moving and ears twitching back and forth, it would hide its face in a corner.

With my 6-foot leather training whip, I would snap at the rear legs until the horse turned around, faced me, and stood still. This was repeated as often as the horse turned and tried to get away.

When the horse finally stood still while facing me, I made it relax more by quietly resting the whip along my side as I continued talking.

After the horse was quiet for a spell, I moved slowly forward until I could stroke its forehead. Lifting the whip, I touched the horse's rump, gave the command, "Come here," and stepped backwards.

Then the horse would follow me out of the pen without a rope. I had just gained its trust. Mission accomplished.

After gaining its trust, I could halter, teach the horse to be led, be tied, and follow commands. If the horse had not previously been mishandled by others, it was only a matter of time before I introduced the blanket and saddle, climbed aboard, and rode away.

A gentle reminder: We must remember that you never teach from only the left side of the horse. Each side of the horse's brain must learn the same lessons if it is to trust you. Approach the horse from the left front with various objects and let it touch them with its nose and lips first.

Move the object slowly along the neck, shoulders, and front legs. Work your way back and touch all parts of the body. Make noise and all kinds of sounds to get the horse to trust that it will not be harmed.

Start by touching it with your riding tack. Then branch out to umbrellas, newspapers, blankets, pots, pans, and any other thing you can find in your environment.

Next approach from the right front and do it all over again. Your simple voice command should be enough to calm the horse. Teaching a horse correctly the first time will resolve, and even prevent most problems you might encounter later on.

Horses receive nearly all commands through sight, sound, skin, and muscle. Never forget it is a reactive animal and cannot reason as you do. My Dad was able to drive his favorite draft horse, Babe, without reins, using only the voice commands: giddy up, gee, haw, whoa, steady, move over, and back up.

Dad loved Babe so much that after switching to tractors, he kept her nearby in the pasture until she died. She served Dad with great devotion from a colt until he was finally able to give her a decent burial. I remember the sadness in his eyes when Babe died.

When a well trained horse sees its trainer, it immediately gives its loyalty and attention to him. That's why you should start talking to your horse right away. Talk to him as though he is a good friend you are going to meet for coffee. The horse will sense your mood through your voice.

Let me try to explain how your horse perceives you, and his relationship to you. Your horse does not realize that it is much larger and stronger than you. He has been trained to believe that you understand and speak his language. That is why he trusts you not to hurt him.

After decades, I still focus on the ground when walking or driving. My wife often says, "Why don't you look around and enjoy the scenery." I admit to her, "I unconsciously look ahead only because in my mind I'm still observing the trail to guide my horse safely. That is my job."

Whenever you are around, the horse's senses are focused on you and what you want done. He doesn't even closely look where you are leading or guiding him. As far as he is concerned, your wish is his command.

A trusting horse believes that you know what you want him to do. You can even ride him until he drops, if you choose. You have seen horses jump from a cliff in the Western movies, and it was real. He is your responsibility. Don't let him down.

A properly trained horse will go out of his way to avoid hurting you. When I was a kid, Dad's horses never intentionally hurt me. However, I discovered early that a good time to stay out of their way was while they were eating and drinking.

When you ride, your horse should be focused on pleasing you. His job is to follow your directions by listening to your voice, following your actions with his eyes, understanding the pull or position of the reins, and feeling the pressure of your legs.

You must function as a team. Your primary job is to observe the trail ahead while your horse carries you along following your commands.

He listens when you sing or talk to other riders. If the reins are loosely held, he will relax with you. At the first sign of tenseness in your body, your horse responds with tenseness in his body. In this regard the horse and rider are one.

Nothing is more sacred than the bond between a horse and a rider. No other creature can ever become so emotionally close to a human as a horse. When a horse dies, the memory lives on, because an enormous part of his owner's heart, soul, and the very existence dies also.

Stephanie M. Thorn

Chapter Seventeen

THINK LIKE A HORSE

Extensive horse training and riding instruction goes beyond the scope of any book. The best advice I can give new riders is this, "If you want to enjoy your horse, you must first learn to think like a horse."

However, following the guidance in this book will certainly put you miles ahead of any other trainer or rider. When you learn how your horse thinks, you will acquire valuable "horse sense."

As with humans, everything the horse learns is self taught. All the trainer does is affect the horse's natural reflexes in such a way that habits become fixed in its mind through repetition.

Since the trainer and the horse understand the same commands, the animal loses fear and becomes obedient. As with a small child, you must wait until the brain is developed enough to retain instruction. This happens when a colt is about two years old.

At that age the colt is mentally and physically capable of receiving instruction. Like young children, they must not become over tired. Start with only 30 minutes of training and slowly expand it to four hours a day. That is plenty of time to get your training accomplished.

There are many additional resources you can find about horses, but for now, we'll stick to the basics taught to me as a teenager. Let's take a look now at the beautiful animal we are talking about.

As we begin, it is important to understand that like humans, the horse has a brain, eyes, ears, nose, mouth, skin, bones, a circulatory system, muscles, nerves, heart, digestive system, and much more.

During training, we work with the structure of skin and bones and muscles that produce their huge strength and power. These systems are controlled by the brain through a superior nervous system.

This produces almost perfect control of its body, giving instant response to any outside incentive. It is because of this highly developed nervous system that the horse became man's favorite beast of burden.

In film and stories, the horse is often given credit for a sort of human intelligence. Don't even entertain the thought. That idea may look and feel good in the movies, but you must forget you ever considered it.

It is man's unique ability to reason that gives him explicit power over the horse and all animals. In this respect, there is a vast gulf between man and the animal kingdom that they cannot ever cross.

To become a great horseman, you must never forget this basic principle: YOUR HORSE SIMPLY CANNOT REASON LIKE A HUMAN. However,

Chapter 17 Think like a Horse

Camel Stretch; Parade Stretch

the horse is not only stronger than we are, but often has a superior sense of seeing, hearing, and smelling.

All of King's training shown in this book was based upon these fundamental understandings.

When handled properly, a horse will place more and more trust in its trainer. This trust is built upon repetitions of acts that are conveyed to the horse's brain by its instincts and not by reasoning power.

When it comes to horses, we judge their behavior from facial expressions and the movements of parts of their body. By observing these, we can see what they are thinking.

Knowledge comes to your horse from the outside world through its keen senses of seeing, hearing, smelling, tasting, and feeling. Since it cannot speak, you must find another way to communicate.

This is first done through the sense of touching, which later is merged into motion and voice. Since you must talk to your horse through signs, do not become irritated if it does not immediately do what you want. Be consistent and remain patient.

I remember when I was a teenager that I became frustrated when my horse did not respond to a trick I was teaching. When I punched the horse on the jaw with my knuckles, I immediately felt the pain. The unaffected horse just stared at me blankly.

While rubbing my painful knuckles, I thought about what had just happened and remembered that a horse cannot reason. That is the exact

Prayer Time; Salute

moment I realized that my only choice was to learn to think like a horse and put myself in its shoes first, last and always.

That axiom worked like a charm, and thereafter, I blamed only myself for miscommunication because I was not making the signs correctly. I learned to study the expression of its eyes, ears, skin, and muscles to see if my intentions were getting through.

Learning to think like a horse was a tremendous breakthrough for me. It allowed me the get into the mind of any horse I was training. I realized the horse did not care about what I was thinking at all. It only reacted by instinct to my outside stimulus.

I hope you stop reading now and dwell for a long moment on what I just revealed. It may be the most important concept you get from this book. **"Learn to think like a horse."**

The following will demonstrate how important this revelation was in shaping the rest of my life. Whenever I am put into a situation demanding immediate action, I always try to put myself into the mind of the person, point of the object, or crux of the problem confronting me.

This forces me to think outside the collection of habitual responses I have stored away in my mind, and look through the eyes of the other person, or viewpoint of the object. I have used this principle throughout my life in widely divergent situations dealing with family, marriage, and work projects.

I even taught this principal to new graduate engineers who worked with me designing complex hydraulic and mechanical systems. I explained it this way:

> Here's the first thing you should know about this pipe. It doesn't care what you think it should do. It can only react to outside forces placed upon it. So you must learn to think like this pipe.

Many of those engineers would privately tell me later, "Bill, I never learned that in college, and it's the best advice I've ever received."

I told them I had learned it after hitting a horse in the jaw with my fist. They always laughed when I said I suffered more pain than the horse, and they always thanked me for the tip.

A complete description of the training of a horse falls beyond the purpose of this book. Therefore, my advice will cover only a few more personal situations to give you confidence in handling your horse.

Teaching a horse to rear upon its hind legs can be very dangerous. Don't try to teach this trick to your horse unless it will be used in a show. Although I have only taught it to a few horses, I have fallen over backwards several times while breaking horses with bad habits.

Use caution the first time you urge the horse forward with your legs while pulling back on the reins. It may result in the horse rearing so high it loses its balance and falls over backwards with you on its back.

Should this happen, you must quickly decide the direction the horse will roll after hitting the ground, and lean sideways out of its path. Trust your balance and legs to tell you where the horse is rolling.

Stay away from the horse's feet if you don't want to be stepped on. It doesn't hurt much in a soft field but can cause major injury on a hard surface. Try to always stay a forearm's length from the horse unless you are putting on the bridle or saddle.

Always be careful when approaching any horse from the rear because it may not see you coming and try to protect itself by kicking. I always let the horse know I am around by talking to it out loud, even before it can hear me.

The Salute

Unless the horse has been trained to see you do things with both eyes, it may react out of fear when you approach it directly from the front. Be alert around a new horse until you test its eye training.

I'll end this chapter by describing how I taught King to lie down on command as part of our stage routine. It takes good planning to accomplish this.

With King haltered and saddled, I led him to soft ground and dropped the left stirrup extra low to keep it from hurting him when he rolled over.

Then I passed a short rope under him and tied both stirrups snuggly together.

I attached a long strap around his left front leg above the hoof, lifted the leg level with his knee, and fastened the strap to the left stirrup. After attaching a long rope to the saddle horn, I ran it through the halter ring and back around the saddle horn.

Standing ahead of King on the left side with rope in hand, I made a powerful sweeping pull which turned his head to the right. When King turned in a circle, I would slacken the rope until he stopped.

Then I would pull again until he dropped to his left knee. Holding the rope tight, I walked around the front to his back and with a strong pull rolled him over onto his left side.

I held the rope tight until he quit struggling to get up. Then I rattled pans and paper around and over him until he lay perfectly still.

King was a smart horse. After a few rope throws, he learned to kneel on his front knees and roll over when I cued him with my riding crop.

Training King to perform on command required lots of patience from both of us. But I will say again, it happened after my major training breakthrough when I began to consistently "Think like a horse."

Chapter Eighteen

BREAKING UP IS HARD TO DO

With the 300 mile horseback trip behind me and the ranch closed until the following spring, I settled into life back on the farm. We put on an occasional show, but not enough to keep busy.

I picked up my job of cooking for the family and keeping the house clean. It was actually a fulltime job since the house was still without any plumbing.

Everything that was carried into the house had to be carried back outside for disposal. This included food, water, and firewood ashes. Everyone still used the king sized outhouse located near the main house.

After a couple of months went by, my Dad said, "Bill, don't you think it's about time you started looking for a job?" He realized that keeping house was a dead end for me. I admit that it hadn't crossed my mind until he asked me that question.

I believed that singing gigs and shows with King would be my future, but there wasn't enough income to keep our show going. I talked it over with

Lew, and he agreed that I should start looking for full time work while working in the show part time.

I began looking for the type of work that would pay enough to build a nest egg to live on while I gave show business another shot. My deepest desire was to one day sing on the stage of the Grand Ole Opry in Nashville, Tennessee.

But, something told me show business was over. That if I moved into a factory job, it would keep me busy for the rest of my life. My instincts were right.

The hardest part was telling King "Goodbye." I knew he wouldn't understand. Sadly, I was right, and after our last seasonal show, I simply hugged him before driving away. He just stood there looking at me with those beautiful trusting eyes.

Times were tough, and it took several months to land a job. I was without a car and had to relocate to another city. I stayed in a rooming house while I worked second shift in a metal finishing factory.

Fond Memories with My Friend King

Chapter 18 Breaking Up Is Hard to Do

The switch from farm life to working second shift in a factory quickly got me down. After six months, I could hardly remember the date, or my own name, so I quit that job.

I accepted another factory job in nearby Kenton, Ohio, working the first shift and never looked back. When they offered a four-year apprentice program in tool design, I jumped at the opportunity.

This led to college and correspondence courses in engineering, which eventually became my goal and my destiny. At 29, I successfully completed the Ohio test and registered as a professional engineer.

Bill the Professional Engineer at Ages 29 and 59

The photograph on the left was published in the *Kenton Times* newspaper announcing my successful registration. On the right is my office 30 years later in Daytona Beach, Florida, as regional manager for a large national environmental consulting company.

When asked how I made the switch from life as a professional cowboy to that of a professional engineer, I grin and say, "Well, I did pray a lot."

During those intervening years, I married the beautiful Phyllis Jean Holycross from Kenton, Ohio. We raised two daughters, Kathryn and Alanna, and a son, Alan, before moving to Florida. Phyllis died very suddenly after nearly 44 years of marriage.

The following year, I was fortunate enough to marry another beautiful Christian lady, Ann Louise (Allebach) Phillips. She had already raised two sons, Scott and Terry. Our shared families of five children have produced 11 grandchildren.

Time passed quickly while I was raising a family and advancing in my engineering career. Sadly, King was not only out of my sight, but out of my mind, too. I must confess that almost 30 years passed before my thoughts turned again to visiting King.

Goodbyes are not forever.
Goodbyes are not the end.
They simply mean I'll miss you
Until we meet again!

Author Unknown

Chapter Nineteen

THE LAST GOODBYE

I decided to try to visit King when he was about 35 years old. I had often told stories about him and the road show, but had not seen King or his owner, Lew Jenkins, since leaving nearly 30 years earlier.

After visiting my Dad in a nearby town, I drove to Lewistown where I grew up and spent the first 21 years of my life. During my youth it had always been a small, peaceful country town.

Just an intersection with a traffic light and a few dozen homes spread around several blocks. It had a grocery store, post office, restaurant, gas station, and the modern 12-grade Washington Township School.

I felt sad and forlorn as I drove through town. Most of the stores had closed and the traffic light was gone. I was struck by the sensation of a time warp when I realized how small the town appeared compared to my boyhood memories.

I stopped at Lew's home near the school and was told he had moved several years earlier. With new directions, I headed back to the intersection and turned east. This road took me past the famous tree where Indian Chief Lewis had signed a peace treaty, thus giving the town its name, Lewistown.

Lew lived alone on a few acres a short distance east of town. It was a very nice place with a long lane leading up to his house. Parking the car, I went to the door and knocked. After the third unanswered knock, I decided to leave and headed down the lane.

King stood alone as I drove by the field where he was pastured. I stopped the car and watched him as he grazed. I began to wonder if he would remember me. After all, it had been almost 30 years since we had been together. I slowly opened the door, stepped out, and walked over to the fence.

I grew a little apprehensive while watching my old friend about 20 yards away. The passing years had taken their toll and he looked frail and gaunt. Not realizing I was near, he continued grazing.

Memories flooded back, and I felt deep emotions begin to well up inside. I softly called out his name. He lifted his head and looked in my direction with ears pointed forward. Tears flowed down my cheeks.

After all those years, King still knew my voice. He approached and put his head over the fence. We stood together for a little while. I thanked him for the hours we trained together, the applause we shared, and wonderful moments on stage.

I told him we were both leaving a legacy through our offspring. Then I kidded him about how much he loved teasing the mares until they submitted to his advances. Man-to-man talk between two old friends.

Chapter 19 The Last Goodbye

 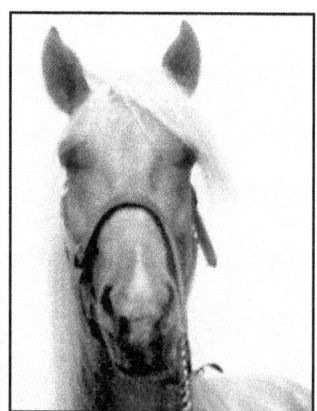

King Grazing; "Goodbye, King"

Being a proud and gentle stallion, he always had his way with them. I reminded him that occasionally he daydreamed about the mares, and that I always made sure he was decent when the ladies visited.

His eyes rolled back as if remembering, and he softly knickered as we laughed about it. I'm sure we reminisced about the many stage shows we had done together. I even recalled the galloping somersault we survived.

Finally, I looked sadly but lovingly at him and said, "Thanks, King. I will never forget you. It's time to say our last goodbye."

My car seemed far away as I made my way back, opened the door, sat down, started the engine, and waved at King for the last time. Then I slowly drove away, knowing we would never see each other again in this life.

More tears drifted down my cheeks as King disappeared from sight in the rear view mirror. I thought to myself as I drove away, "If horses have a heaven there is one thing I know; my friend King has a wonderful home."

Tears still fall as I write down this memory of seeing King for the last time. There is one truth I have learned and wish to share: "Loving a horse will enrich your soul and break your heart!"

Smilin' Bill and his Wonder Horse King
My Fondest Memory

Chapter Twenty

WITHOUT HEROES

Without heroes, we're all plain people and don't know how far we can go.
                                        Bernard Malamud

One by one, our heroes have disappeared, and it seems that there is no one left to blaze the moral trail. Many in our younger generations seem lost! We must hope and pray God will lift up new heroes for our young people to follow.

We need heroes to help us through the dreadful times that occur. Real people with vision, values and principles based upon our God-given rights of life, liberty, and the pursuit of happiness.

People of my generation had a generous helping of heroes to choose from. I naturally gravitated to the Western cowboy heroes like Gene Autry and Roy Rogers. They set high moral and ethical standards for all the kids of the Great Depression to live by.

The good guys wore white hats and the bad guys dressed in black. Even though we knew at the start of the movie that the hero would save the pretty lady in distress, we waited anxiously during each show.

The moral values we learned were priceless.

My personal singing style was more like Gene Autry than Roy Rogers, so Gene became my idol. Since everyone had an idol they looked up to when I was young, this was not a problem. Today is another story, and I see no icon for kids to emulate.

Gene used the Melody Ranch Hands with their gentle Western tempo as backup musicians. They highlighted his soft easy voice as he sang stories of the old west and of cowboy life on the prairie.

On the other hand, Roy sang best with the Sons of the Pioneers, who were famous in their own right. His tempo was faster than Gene's with a little more of the Hollywood style in his presentation.

It's interesting to note that Gene was my singing mentor, while King looked a lot like Roy's famous horse, Trigger. Gene grew up in Oklahoma while Roy and I grew up in Ohio. It is easy to grasp how they both influenced my childhood and career plans.

Reflecting on decades of heroes I have known, no one comes closer than Gene Autry to the American image of patriotism, goodness, justice, and good over evil. Following his great career gave me values and ideals that I adhered to throughout my life.

During his career, Gene Autry made 93 movies, 640 recordings, and starred in hundreds of television shows and radio programs. He is the only performer to be awarded five points on his Hollywood

Walk of Fame star for his recordings, motion pictures, radio, television, and live performances.

During the 1930's, Gene Autry had a big impact on the city of Kenton, Ohio, located only a few miles from my home. During the great depression of the 1930's, breadlines grew long, and one by one, the local factories in Kenton became silent.

In 1937, Gene selected the Kenton Hardware Company to manufacture all of his cast iron toy six shooters. They sold like hot cakes, and the factory hired so many workers that Gene is credited with saving Kenton from becoming a ghost town.

When Gene Autry visited the factory in 1938, he posed with Monette Whitmore for a picture. Autry joked with her that he made a penny off each of the

Monette Whitmore and Gene Autry with Cap Pistol

toy pistols she made. Her photograph with Gene is a treasured memento.

Gene went on to become one of Hollywood's biggest stars and America's favorite singing cowboy. By 1939, the company had sold two million of the Gene Autry Repeating Cap Pistols for the retail price of 50 cents.

To honor Gene, the Hardin County Chamber of Commerce holds a Gene Autry Days Festival in the City of Kenton during the month of June. In 2004, it commissioned a mural to be done of Autry astride Champion showing his toy cap guns, and the Kenton Hardware Company in the background.

The mural is painted across the side of a three story building in downtown Kenton, and will startle you as you drive into town from the west.

Bill in Kenton City Park Honoring Gene Autry

Chapter 20 Without Heroes

Bill in front of the Gene and Champion Mural

The mural and park are located on the corner of West Franklin and Market Streets across from the movie theater where Gene appeared during his visit. I was thrilled to be photographed in the park in front of the mural on a recent visit.

An extensive display of Gene's cap guns can be seen at the Hardin County Museum in Kenton.

Gene Autry's horse, Champion, and Roy Rogers' horse, Trigger, became stars in their own right with loyal fan clubs. Gene and Roy often seemed to prefer their Hollywood horses over their female co-stars. Of course, this brought much teasing by the girls and tickled the young movie-struck boys.

Johnny Mack Brown was already famous as a Western movie star and was the featured attraction during the Michigan State Fair in 1950. King was so 'Hollywood' gorgeous that Johnny chose King to ride in his shows at the fair in lieu of shipping his movie horse, Rebel, from California. Johnny was a good horseman and said he really enjoyed working

Johnny Mack Brown and Rebel — Autographed Photos

Chapter 20 Without Heroes

with King in front of the grandstand during the fair.

Johnny Mack Brown's Hollywood career spanned more than 25 years and included about 165 films. He was also an outstanding athlete and was selected as the most valuable player for the 'Bamas of Alabama when they beat the Washington Huskies in the 1926 Rose Bowl game.

There were many Western movie heroes, other than Gene Autry, Roy Rogers, and Johnny Mack Brown who helped us grow up—stars like Hopalong Cassidy, Dale Evans, Tom Mix, John Wayne, Will Rogers, Tex Ritter, Buck Jones, the Lone Ranger, Gary Cooper, Red Ryder, Glenn Ford, and Ronald Reagan, along with dozens more just like them.

In the midst of all our Great Depression misery, the Saturday night movie took us out of the solemn reality around us for an hour or so. It let us dream big dreams of a better tomorrow waiting just around the bend.

Oh, how we dreamed of riding off into the sunset with our favorite cowboy star. There is no way to tell the scope and number of positive attitudes fostered among the fans by these cowboy movies and their heroes.

Think of all the virtue spread across this barren land during those many years of depression, hunger, and fear. Just imagine all the hope generated by our parents when they sent us kids to the weekly movie.

It is easy for those of us who were youngsters during the Great Depression and World War II to skip over the hardship our parents endured just to keep food on the table every day. These are our true heroes, and we must never forget their sacrifice.

Thank you, God, for gracing us with real heroes!

ON A PERSONAL NOTE

My deceased wife, Phyllis Jean Holycross, grew up in Kenton, Ohio, home of the Kenton Hardware Company. It is her Aunt Monette Whitmore whose picture was taken with Gene Autry when he visited in 1938.

Robert Bailey was a high school friend to Phyllis. He became a collector of authentic Gene Autry cap pistols. Bob not only helped pioneer the Gene Autry Days Festival in Kenton but also lent an extensive collection of his Gene Autry cap guns to the Hardin County Museum.

His display of cap guns is one block north of the courthouse on Main Street in Kenton. Displayed also is a huge collection of classic toys that were produced by the world-famous Kenton Hardware Company.

AFTERWORD

*Show me the man you honor,
and I will know what kind of a man you are.*
                                    Thomas Carlyle

Gene Autry Was My Hero

I have requested his hymn, "Rounded Up In Glory," to be played at the end of my earthly trail.
                                    The Author

APPENDIX A

GENE AUTRY'S COWBOY CODE

* The cowboy must never shoot first, hit a smaller man or take unfair advantage.
* He must never go back on his word or a trust confided in him.
* He must always tell the truth.
* He must be gentle with children, the elderly and animals.
* He must not advocate or possess racially or religiously intolerant ideas.
* He must help people in distress.
* He must be a good worker.
* He must keep himself clean in thought, speech, action and personal habits.
* He must respect women, parents and his nation's laws.
* The cowboy is a patriot.

APPENDIX B

KING'S BREASTCOLLAR PRESERVED

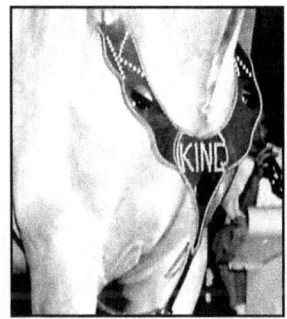

King's Red Breastcollar

My sincere gratitude goes to Jerry McLaughlin of Belle Center, Ohio, for preserving King's red leather breastcollar and bridle after Lew Jenkins died. These may be the only remaining artifacts of King and The Diamond J Road Show.

Fashioned from small silver conchos, the noble name "KING" adorns the breastplate. Emblazoned along both sides of the neck is the large initial "K" with five large silver conchos that add sparkle to the red leather that highlighted King's golden color.

Lew Jenkins hand tooled the breast collar in his leather shop in Lewistown, along with the bridle and surcingle. He was a man of many talents.

APPENDIX C

I'M GONNA RIDE THAT TRAIL TO HEAVEN

Lyrics by William A. Cummins—1947
Transcribed by Ted Stedman—2011

(Verse)

I'm gonna ride that trail to heaven, bye and bye.
I'm gonna ride that long, long trail into the sky.
And there I'll meet my neighbors, one and all.
We will be together for the roundup in the fall.

The Lord has whip and rope and gun
to help Him in the fight,
to straighten out the cowboys
who somehow can't go right.

I'm gonna ride that trail to heaven, bye and bye,
and live on the ranch of the Lord.

(Refrain)

Get along, little pony,
we mustn't make the others wait.
Get along, little pony,
or we'll be left outside the gate.

A musical transcription is available from
CAI Publishing: www.caipublishing.net
or the author, wacummins@clearwire.net

APPENDIX D

WHY DO COWBOYS WEAR HIGH HEELS?

Never squat while wearing your spurs.
                              Will Rogers

As a lad, the first question I asked after seeing a Western movie was, "Why do cowboys wear high-heeled boots?" I was told it began hundreds of years ago when riders were badly injured or even killed when dragged by a frightened horse after being thrown off with their boot caught in the stirrup.

To protect the riders, sturdy tapered high heels were attached to their boots to keep them from slipping through the stirrups. They also added stitching to the tall leather shaft of the boots to give them extra wear, strength, and leg protection.

To keep people's feet out of dusty streets and open drainage, the high-heeled boots were then adapted for walking by the general population. During the eighteenth century, streets improved. Most men gave up wearing high-heeled boots, except for the cowboys.

Steel toes were added to the boots to protect a rider's toes from being crushed by the horse's weight when he stands on a rider's foot, and he will, at some point, stand on your foot.

Today, cowboy boots are worn by men as a statement of rugged individualism. Women wear high-heeled boots and shoes for the extra height and the chic look it adds to their legs and ankles.

APPENDIX E
AN OLD COWBOY'S TOMBSTONE

Russell J. Larsen's headstone is in the Logan City Cemetery, Logan, Utah. He died without knowing he would win the 'Coolest Headstone' contest.

TWO THINGS I LOVE MOST,
GOOD HORSES AND BEAUTIFUL
WOMEN, AND WHEN I DIE I HOPE
THEY TAN THIS OLD HIDE OF MINE
AND MAKE IT INTO A LADIES RIDING
SADDLE, SO I CAN REST IN PEACE
BETWEEN THE TWO THINGS I LOVE MOST.

APPENDIX F
RESOURCES

You can find even more specific information on horse training, riding, and therapy by seeking advice from professionals. To be successful you must endeavor to collect all the "how tos" in your areas of interest.

These resources are recommended to get you started:

HOPE REINS, INC.
Therapeutic Riding Center at Marcody Ranch, 3804 Pioneer Trail, New Smyrna Beach, FL 32168. Visit http://www.hopereinsinc.org for more information. Hope Reins is a member of the North American Riding for the Handicapped Association (NARHA).

FUNDAMENTAL TRAINING FOR HORSE & RIDER
Nine videos by Gary Stauffer, Extension Educator, University of Nebraska, 128 North 6th Street, Suite 100, O'Neill, NE 68763. Telephone: 402.336.2760 or email at gstauffer1@unl.edu. For video presentations: http://www.extension.org/pages/11604/fundamental-training-for-horse-rider.

KING AND THE COWBOY
This book is the foremost resource dealing with the personal training of a stage or show horse. All skills covered in this book were taught by expert horsemen through hands-on training.

For detailed instructions, contact the author, William A. Cummins, by email: wacummins@clearwire.net; or CAI Publishing at http://www.caipublishing.net.

APPENDIX G

OTHER BOOKS BY AUTHOR

It isn't what a book costs; it's what it will cost if you don't read it. The book you don't read won't help.
                                                                Jim Rohm

WILLIAM A. CUMMINS is a highly acclaimed award winning author. All of his books are available and recommended for your reading enjoyment:

- *LIFE IS SEXUALLY TRANSMITTED — Why Marriage Is All About Cleaving* is a highly praised human relationship story straight out of Genesis that will warm your heart.
- *THE FORGOTTEN — Volume One: The Forgotten "Flag;" The Forgotten "War;" The Forgotten "Victory"* is an award-winning Korean War narrative with foxhole stories written in the veterans' own words.

CAI Publishing was founded by the author in 2006. It is called The Home of Celebrity Authors because its goal is to give all aspiring writers a vivid powerful publishing experience.

Review and order these books at
http://www.caipublishing.net

QUICK ORDER FORM

Email orders: info@caipublishing.net *Fax orders:* 1.440.306.0649
Telephone orders: 1.386.383.5198.

Postal orders: Send to CAI Publishing
807 Black Duck Drive, Suite A
Port Orange, FL 32127-4726
USA

Please send the following books from *http://www.caipublishing.net*. I understand that I may return them for a full refund—for any reason, no questions asked.

_____   _____
_____   _____
_____   _____

Send FREE information on
[ ] Other books   [ ] Speaking   [ ] Coaching   [ ] Consulting

Name: _____
Address: _____
City: _____ State: _____ Zip: _____
Telephone: _____
Email: _____

Sales tax: Florida add sales tax at point of delivery for books shipped.
Shipping and Handling: **US:** $6.00 for the first book or disk and $3.00 for each additional product. ***International:*** $15.00 for first book or disk and $7.50 for each additional product (estimate).

Payment method: [ ] Check   [ ] Visa   [ ] Discover   [ ] Master Card
Card number: _____
Name on card: _____
Expiration Date: _____ / _____   Amount approved: $_____

All credit cards will be processed through PayPal.

www.ingramcontent.com/pod-product-compliance
Lightning Source LLC
Chambersburg PA
CBHW071434160426
43195CB00013B/1894